SANTANA

dance of the Rainbow Serpent

volume three *Spirit*

Transcriptions by Hemme Luttjeboer
Project Manager: Aaron Stang
Music Editors: Aaron Stang & Colgan Bryan
Cover Art: Michael Rios and Anthony Machado
    of Heaven Smiles Art Productions
Book Layout: Frank Milone & Joann Carrera

S0-DVC-485

ALL I EVER WANTED

Words and Music by
CARLOS SANTANA, CHRIS SOLBERG
and ALEX LIGERTWOOD

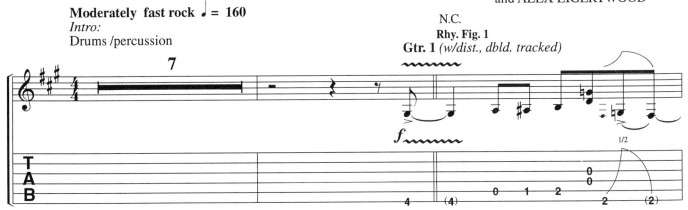

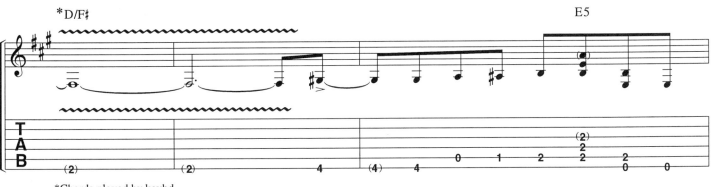

*Chords played by keybd.

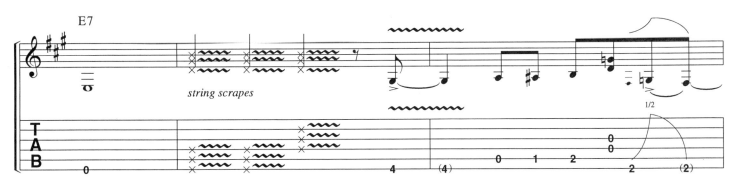

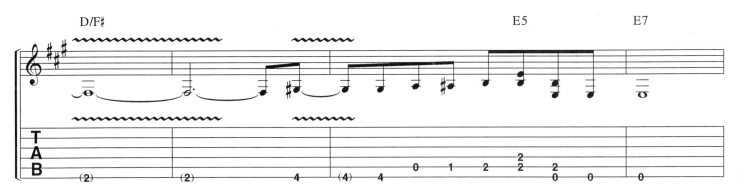

All I Ever Wanted - 13 - 1
PG9540

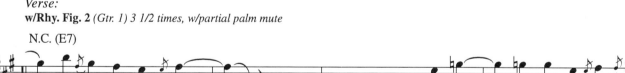

Verse:
w/Rhy. Fig. 2 *(Gtr. 1) 3 1/2 times, w/partial palm mute*

es I re- mem- ber,_____ where the la - dies are so tend- er._____
(3.) See additional lyrics

_____ I can choose_____ and can't com - plain._____

8

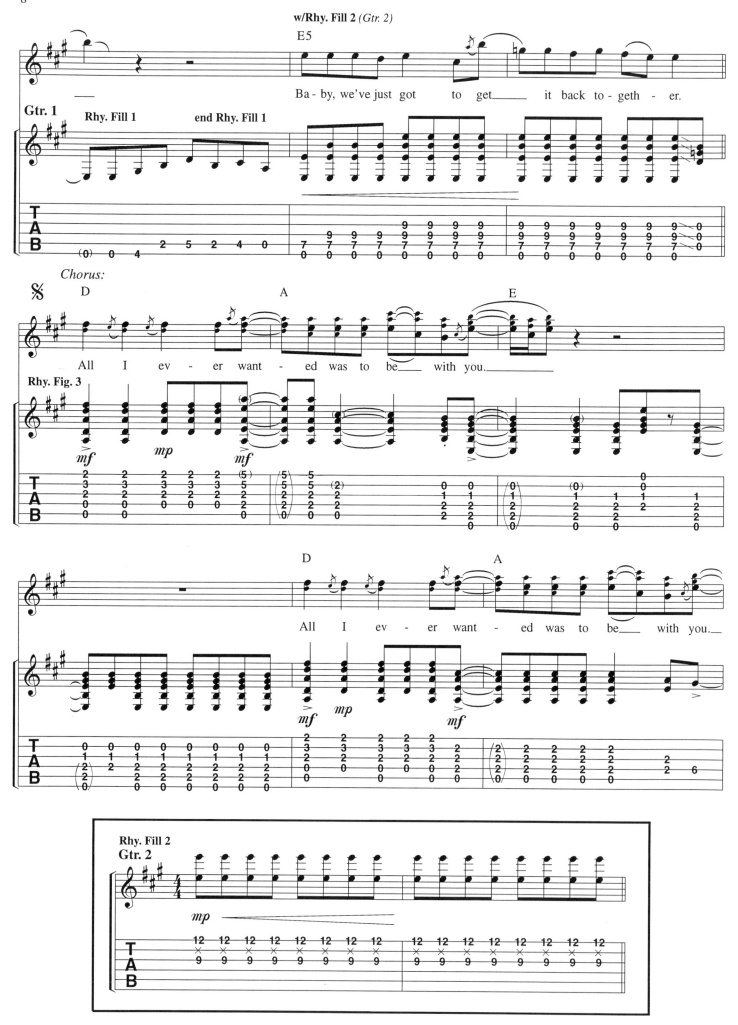

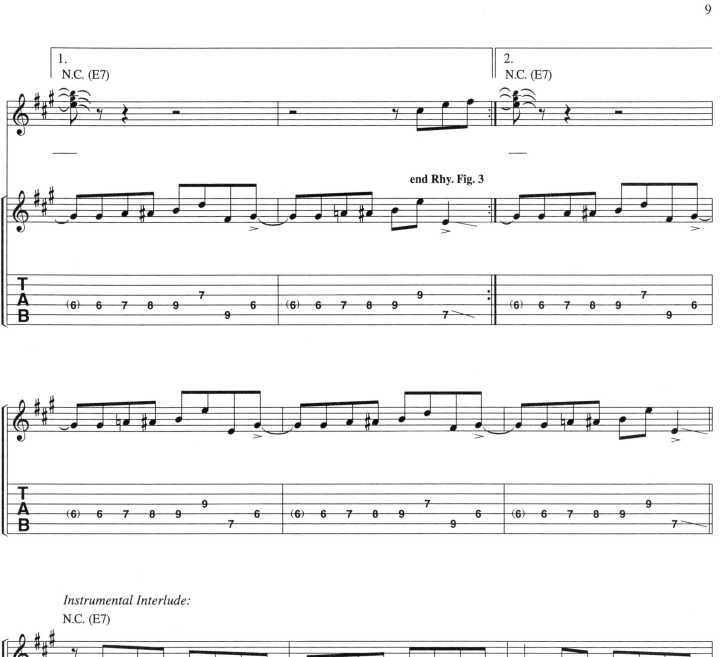

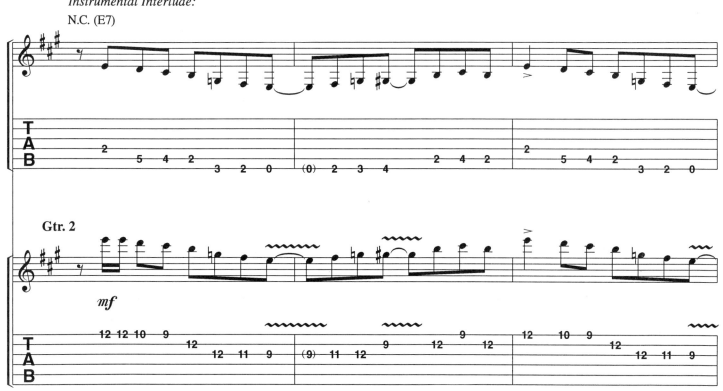

10

All I Ever Wanted - 13 - 6
PG9540

*Chords played by keybd.

string scrapes

w/Rhy. Fig. 1 (Gtr. 1)

Gtr. 2

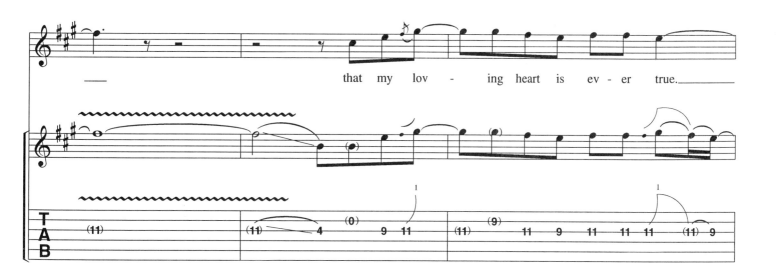

that my lov - ing heart is ev - er true._____

Please come back_____ to where___ you be - long._____

w/Rhy. Fill 1 *(Gtr. 1)*

Band tacet
E5

Gtr. 1

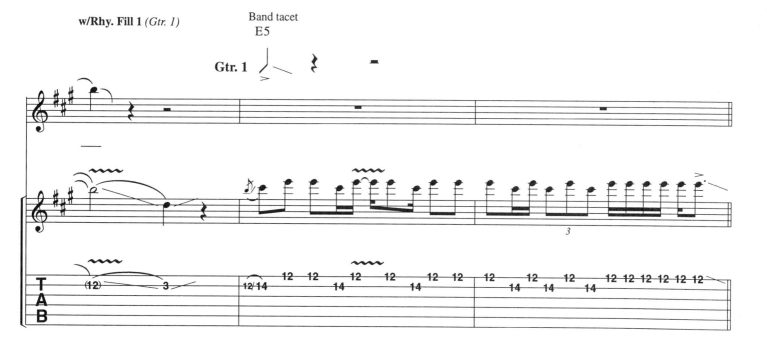

Verse 2:
I've just got to get it through to you
That my loving heart is ever true.
Please come back to where you belong.
Girl, you got to know I'll never do you wrong.
(To Chorus:)

HANNIBAL

Words and Music by
CARLOS SANTANA, ALEX LIGERTWOOD,
ALAN PASQUA and RAUL REKOW

Moderately fast ♩ = **132**
Intro:
Gtr. 1 *(Acoustic nylon string)*

Gtr. 2 *(Acoustic dbld. by electric)*

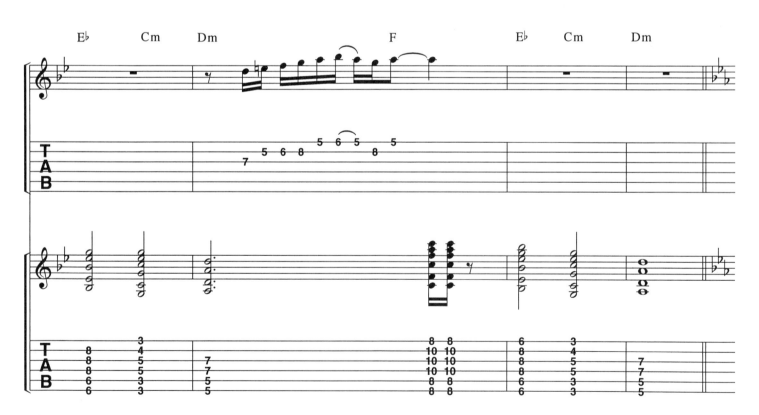

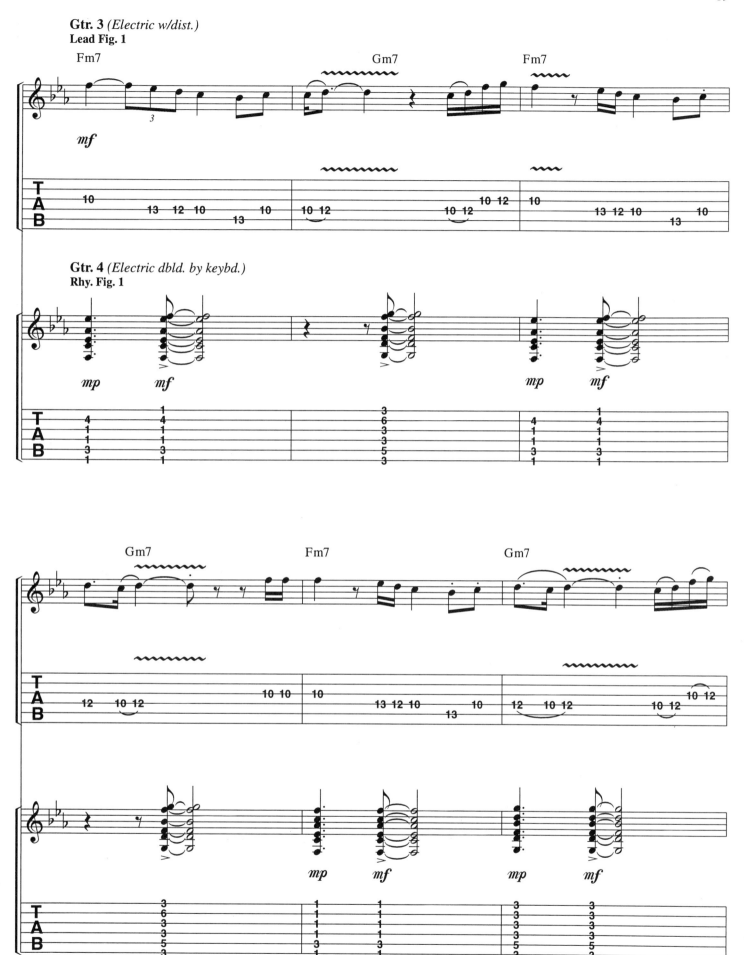

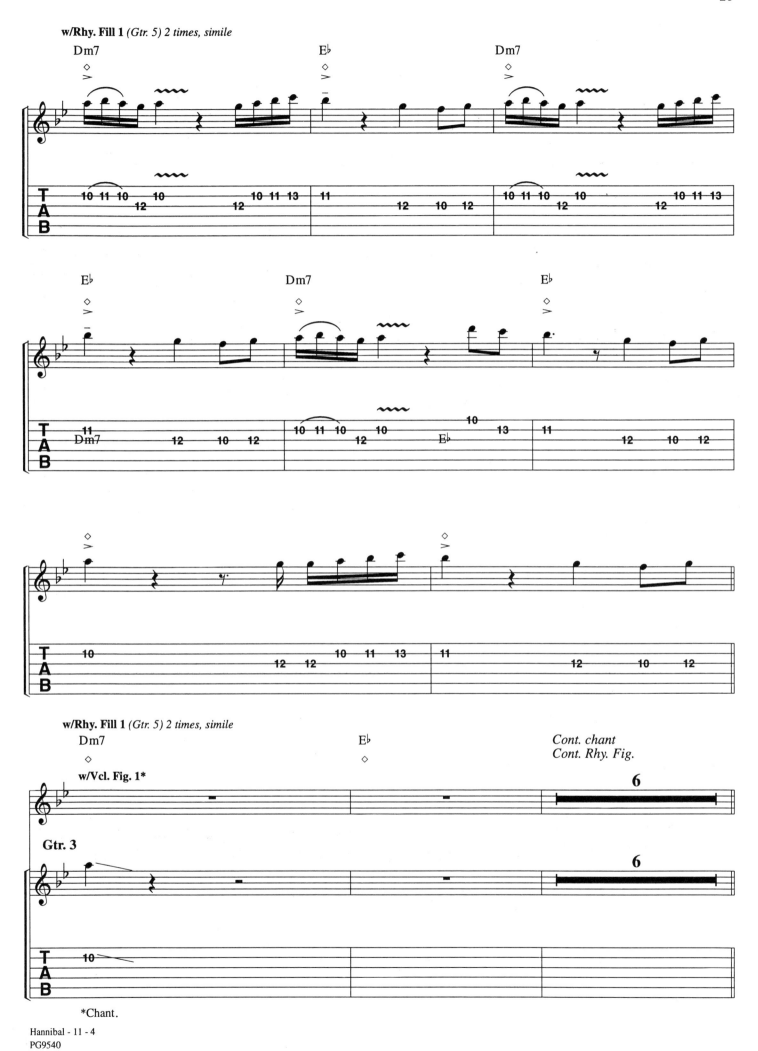

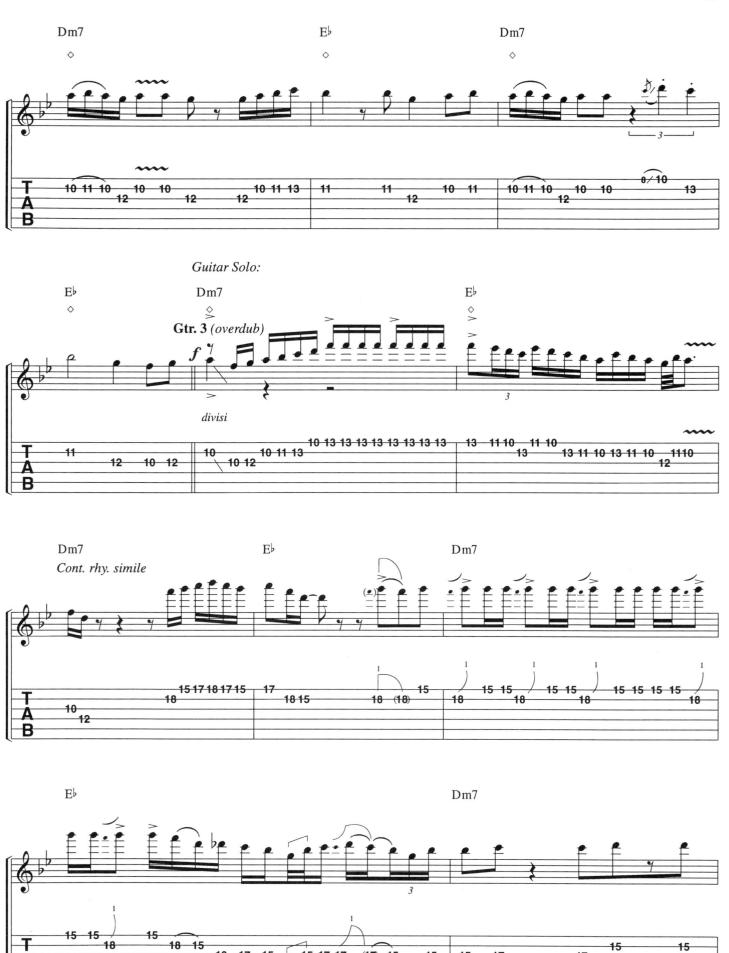

26

Hannibal - 11 - 9
PG9540

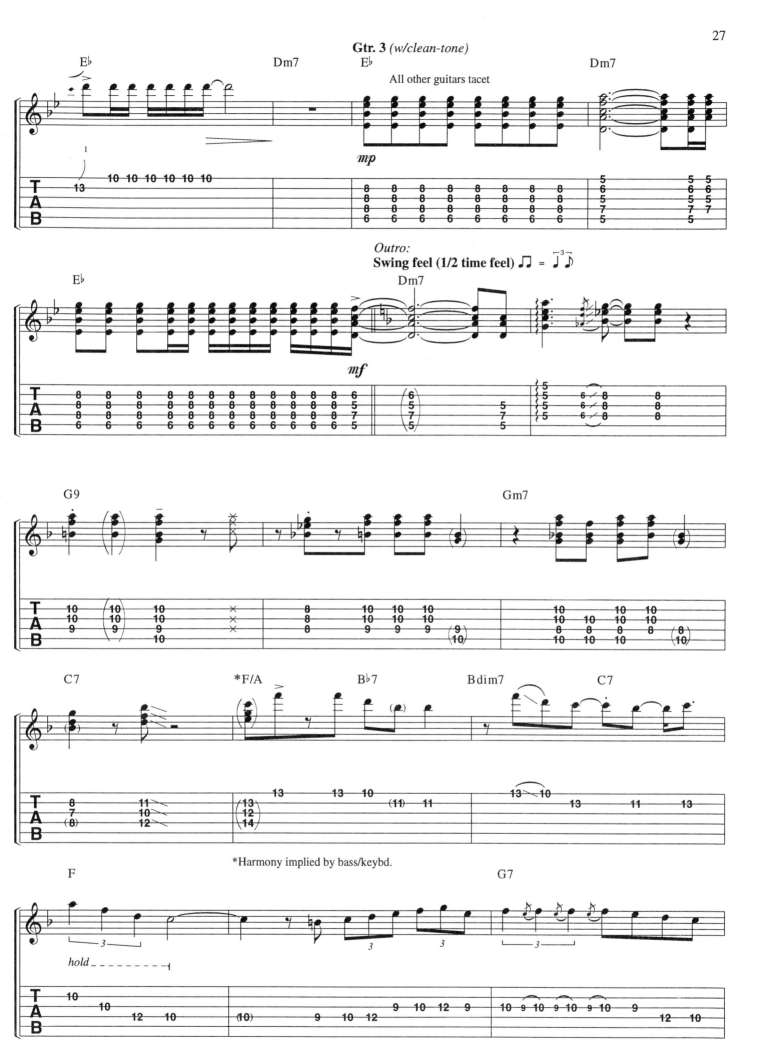

28

BRIGHTEST STAR

Words and Music by
CARLOS SANTANA and ALEX LIGERTWOOD

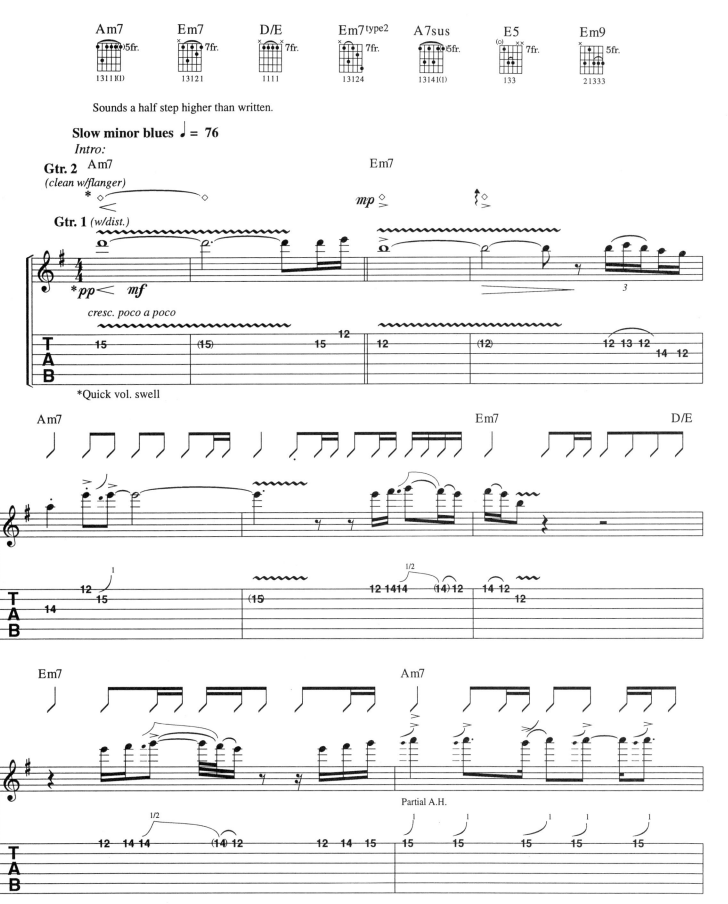

Sounds a half step higher than written.

Slow minor blues ♩ = 76

Intro:

*Quick vol. swell

oh,____ I miss you so.__ Please__

__ come back to me. I need your love,____ oh, oh, oh, ba - by,

ev - er so more,__ yeah,____ yeah.____ Come back now.____

Bring__ your sweet love back to me.____ I can't__

__ do with- out her, no. No, no, no, no, no, no, no, no, no, no.

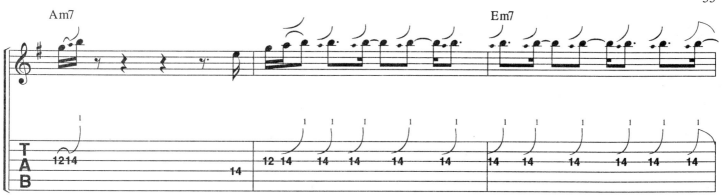

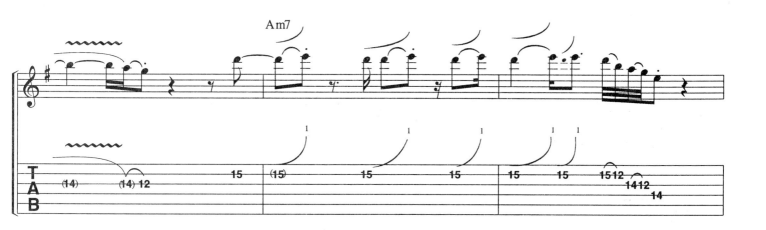

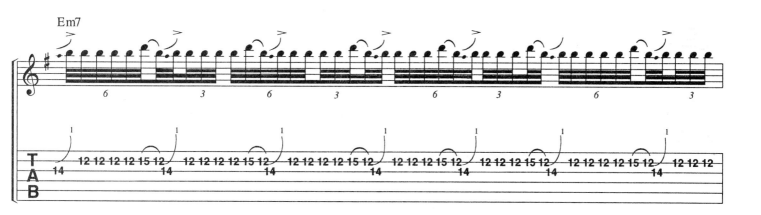

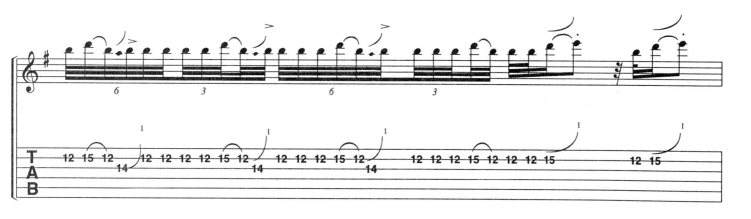

Won't_ you come_back, please, oh, please._ Please, plea, please._

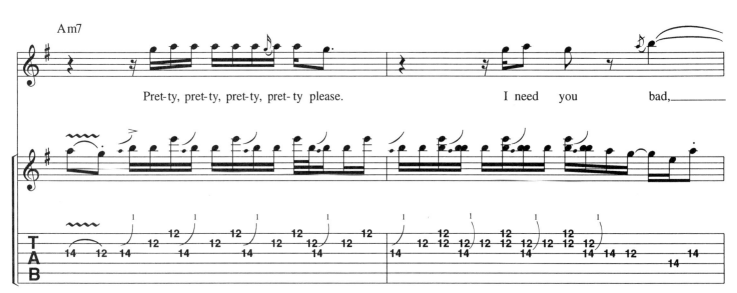

Pret-ty, pret-ty, pret-ty, pret-ty please. I need you bad,_____

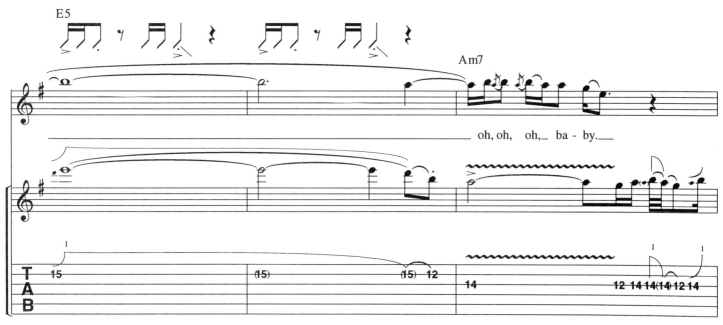

oh, oh, oh,_ ba - by._

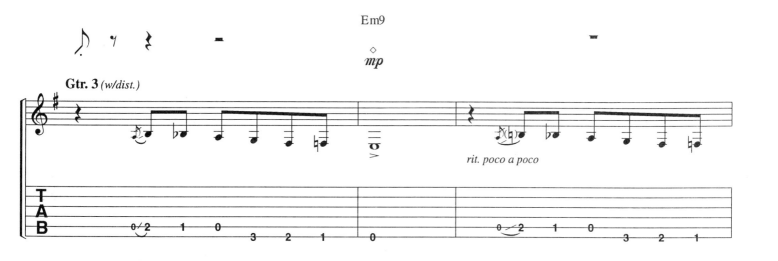

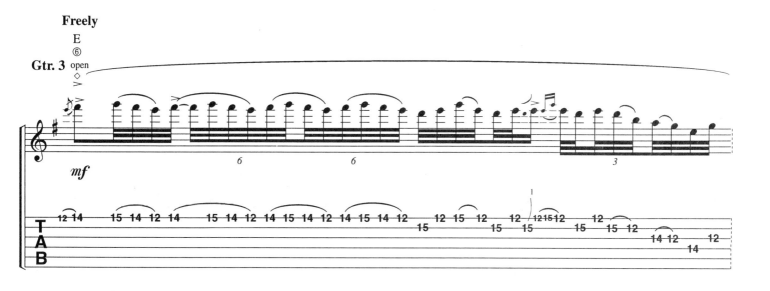

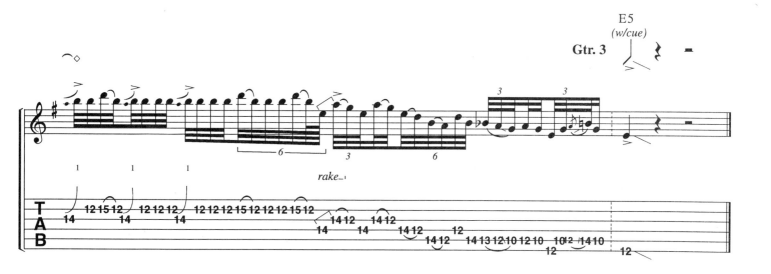

WINGS OF GRACE

Words and Music by
CARLOS SANTANA and CHESTER THOMPSON

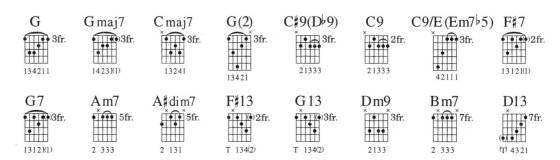

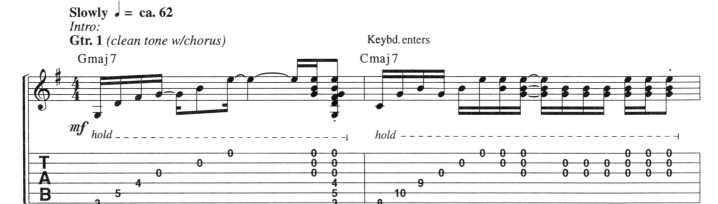

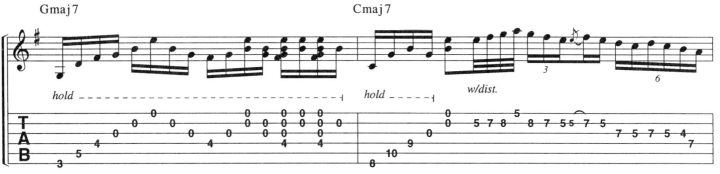

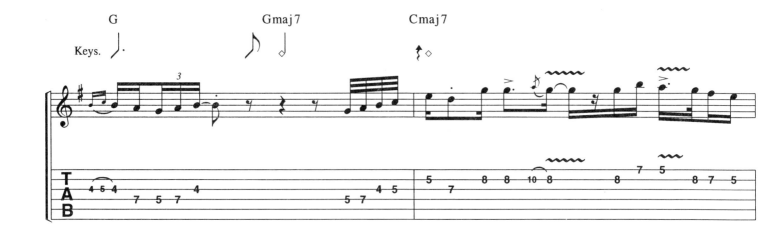

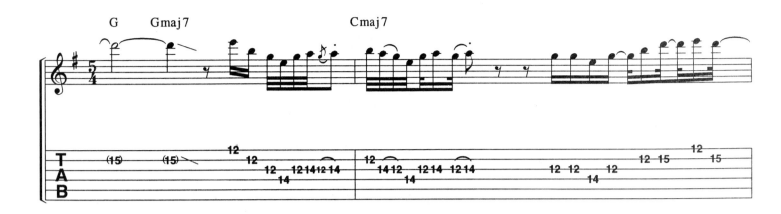

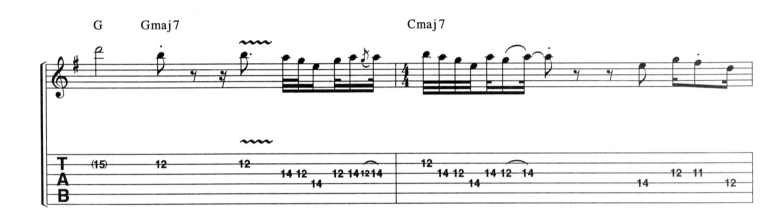

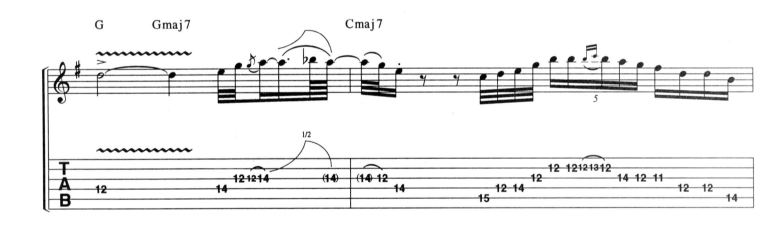

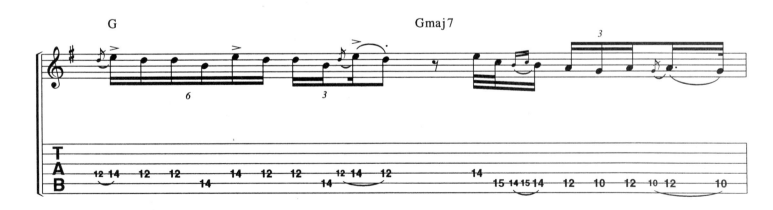

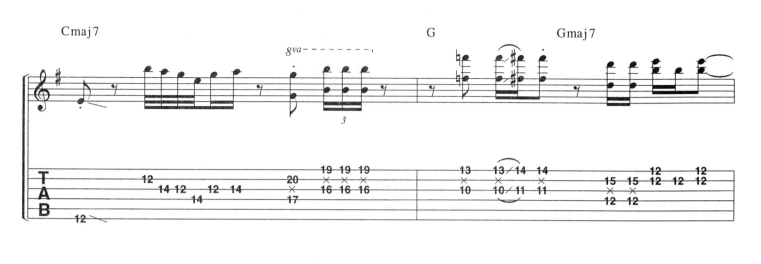

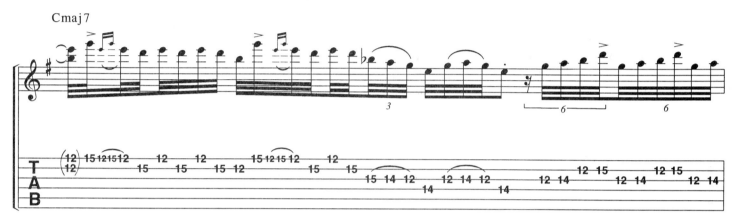

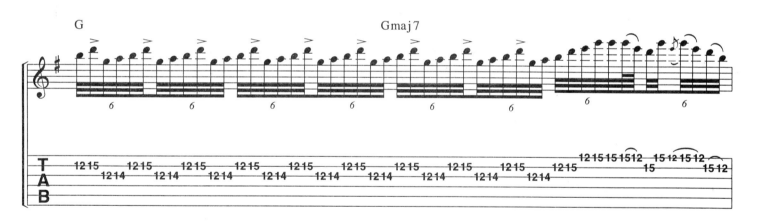

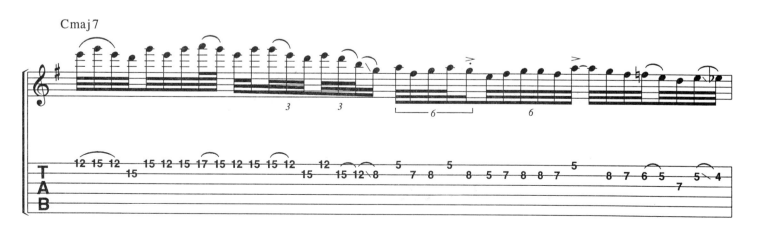

42

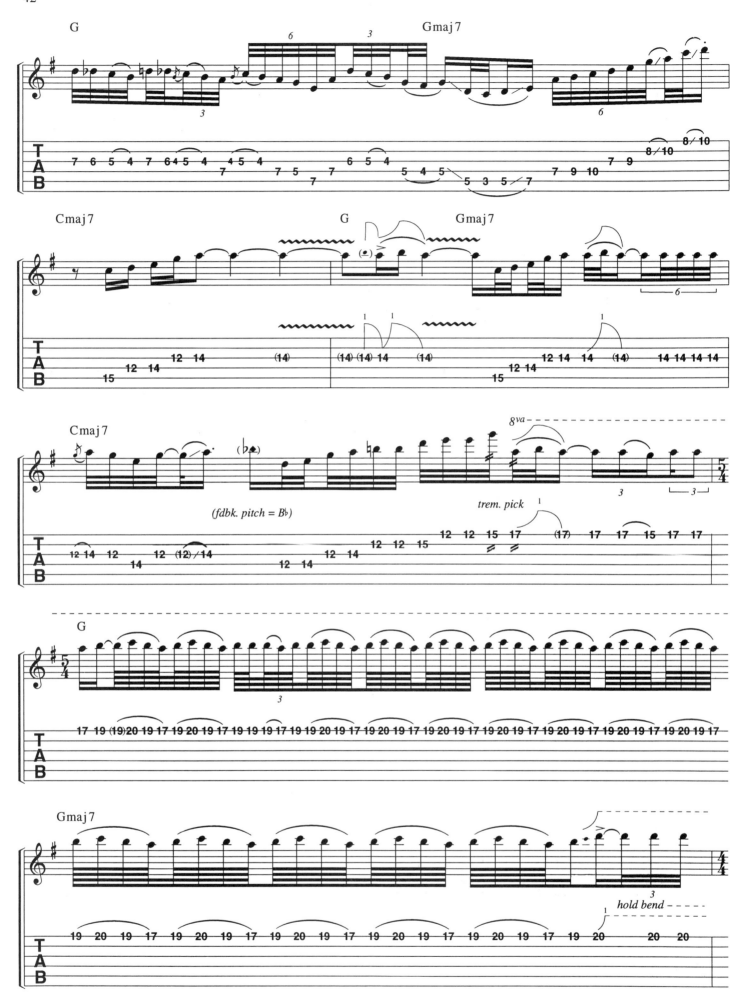

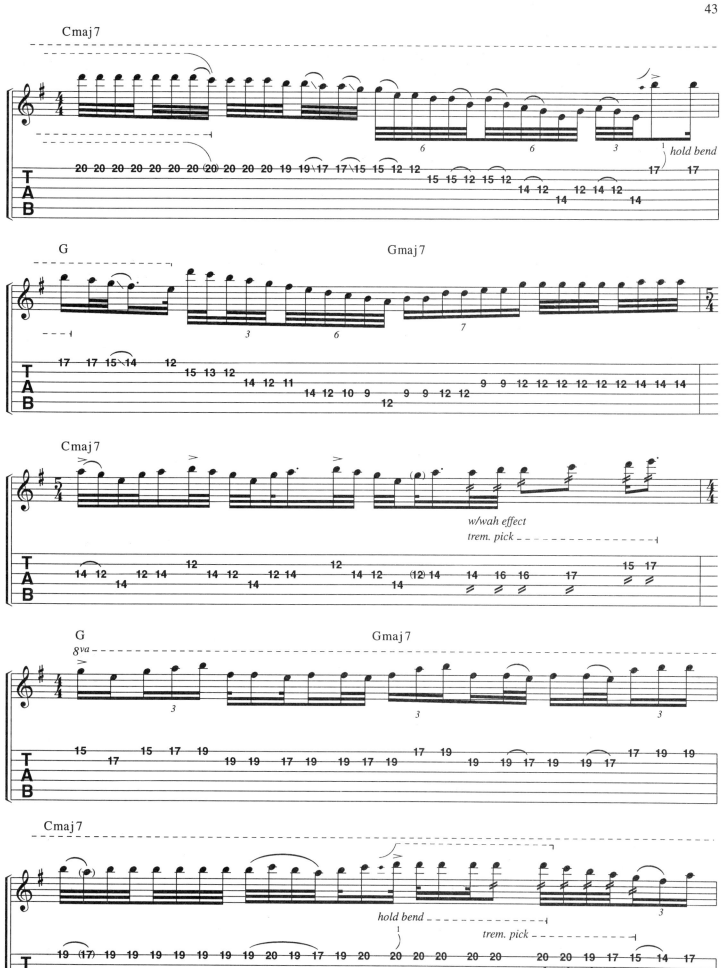

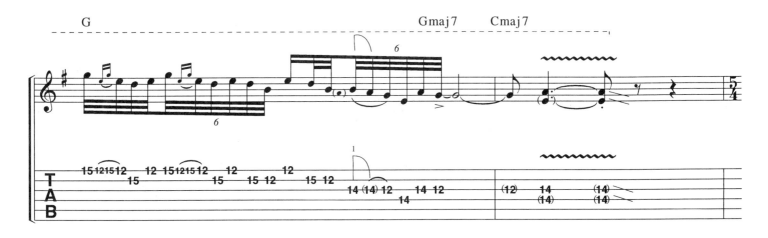

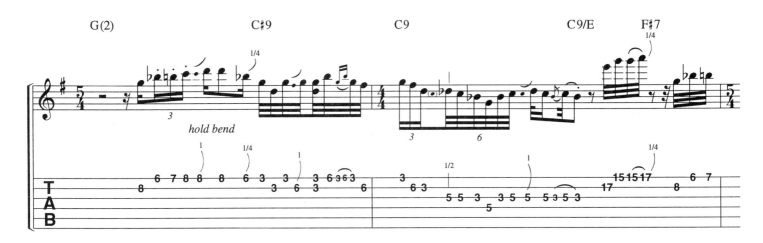

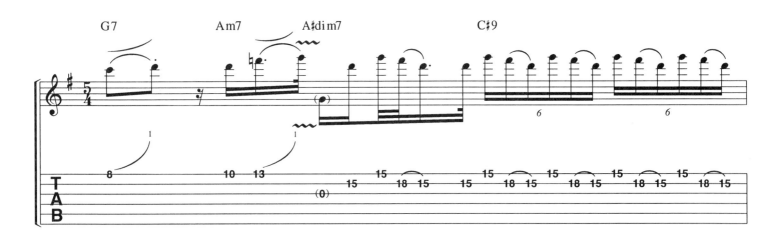

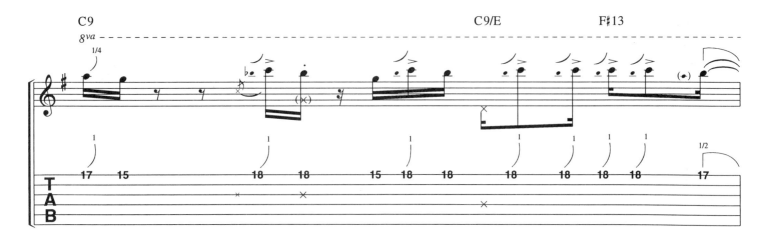

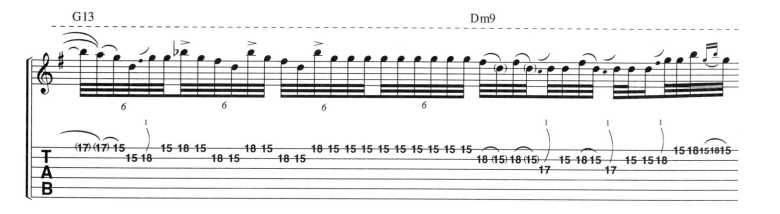

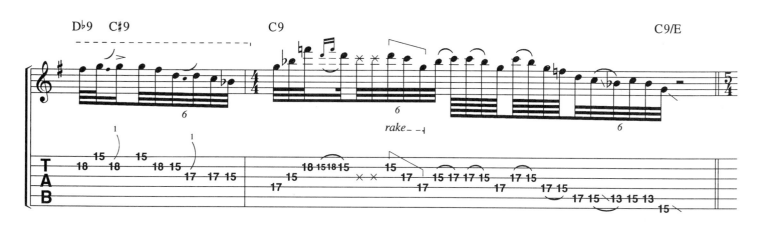

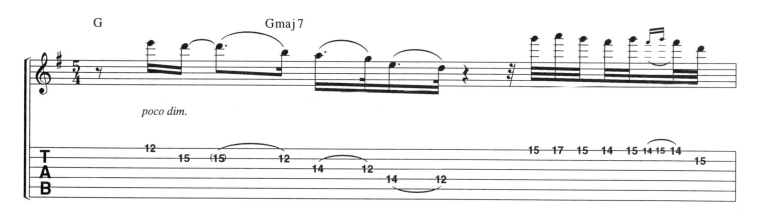

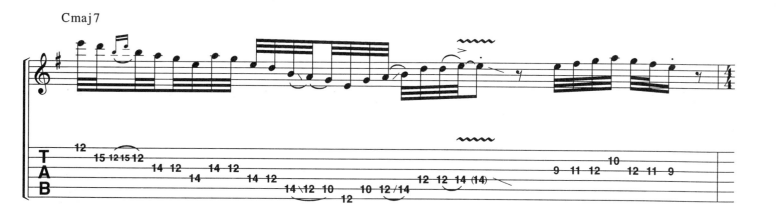

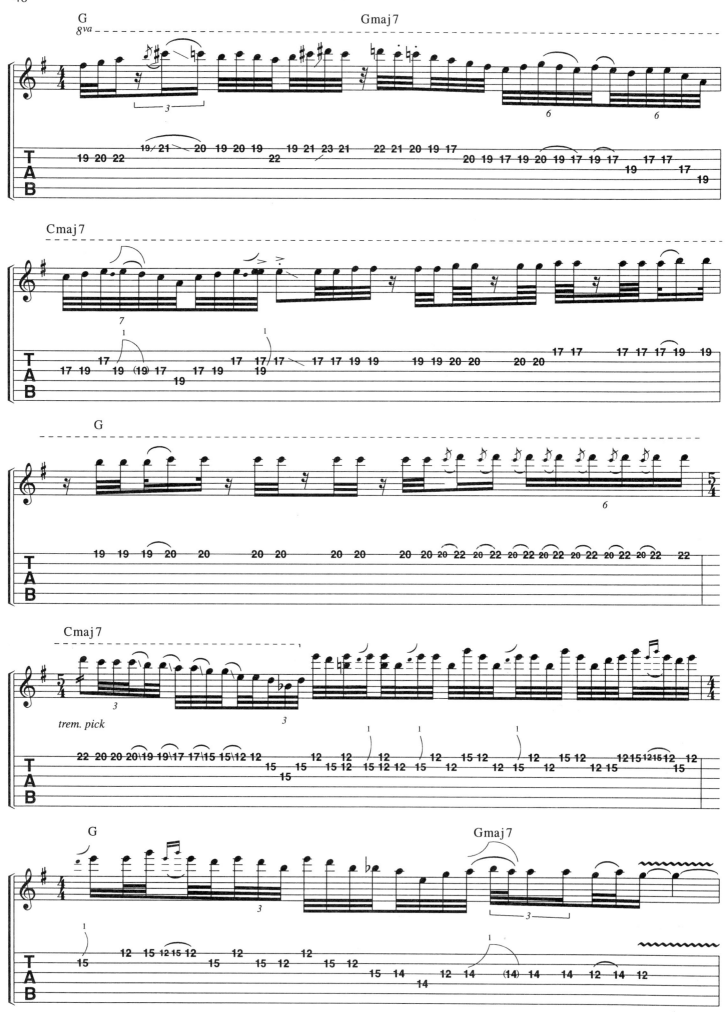

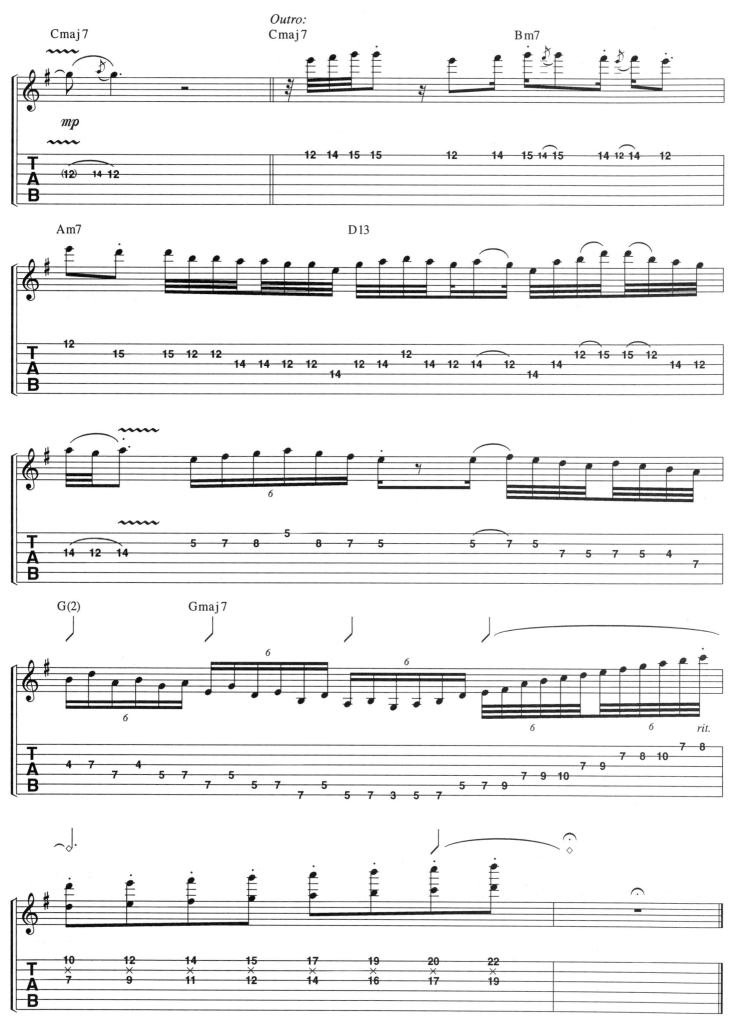

SE ENI A FE L'AMO-KERE KERE

By BABATUNDE OLATUNJI

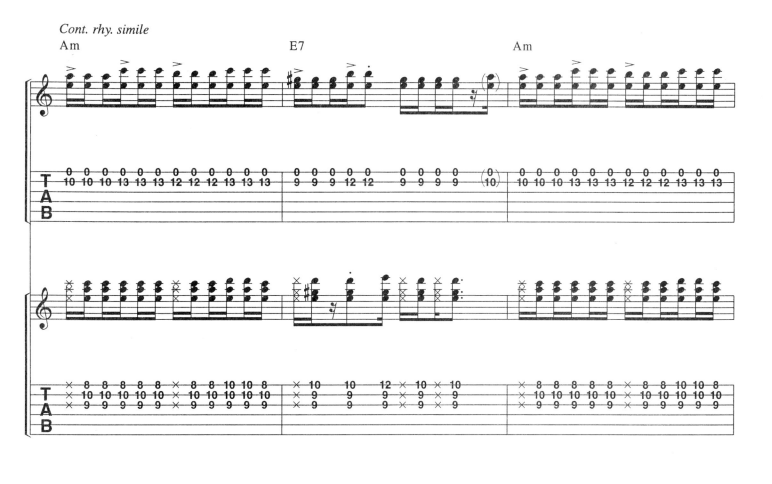

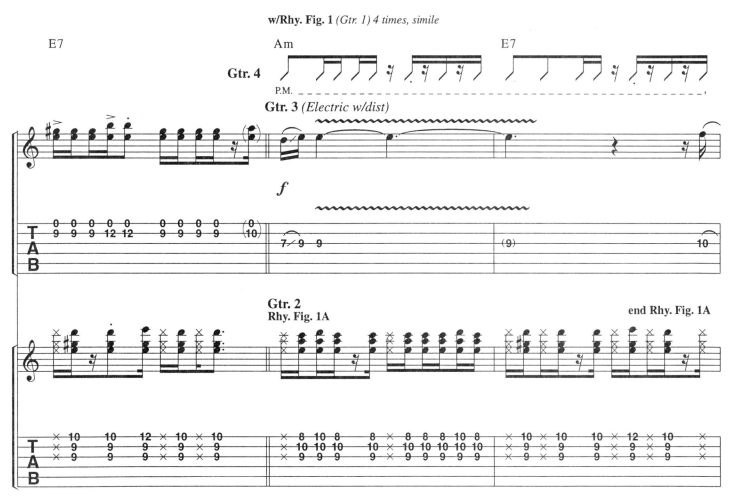

w/Rhy. Fig. 1A *(Gtr. 2) 3 times, simile*

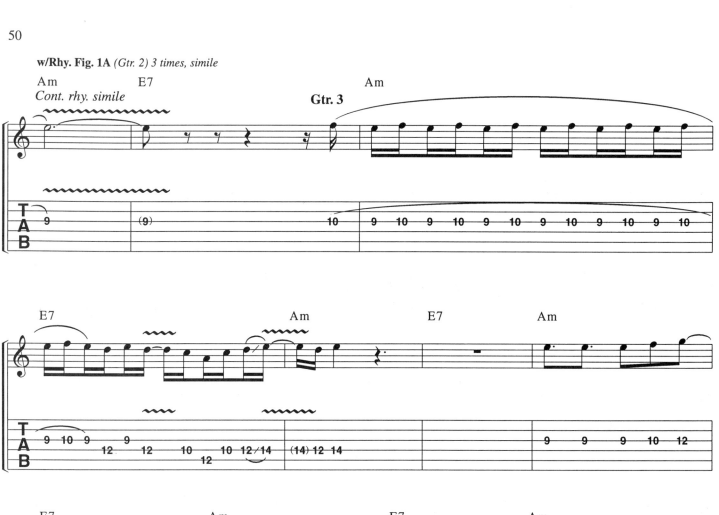

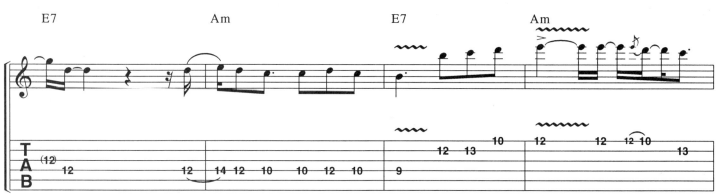

1. S'en - ia fe - l'a -

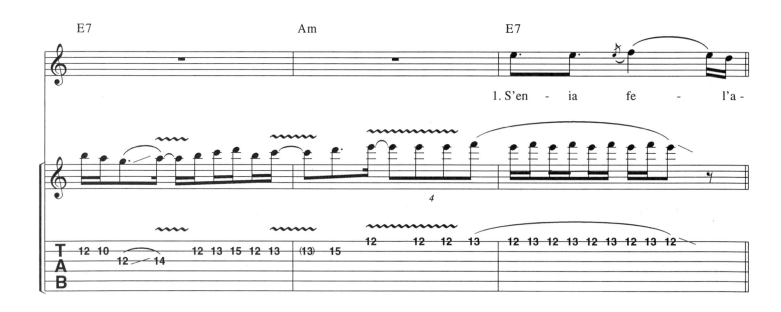

Verse 1:

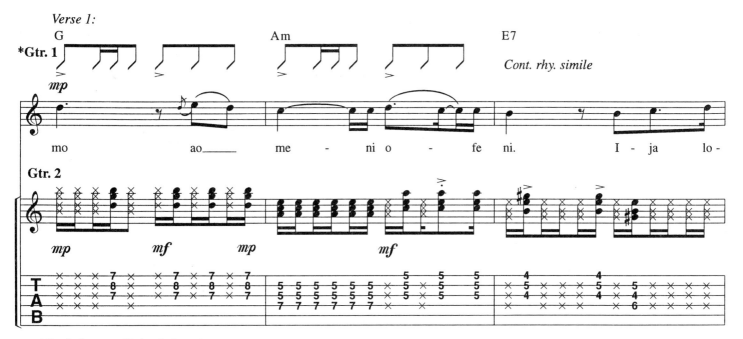

*Gtr. 1 plays type II chords throughout.

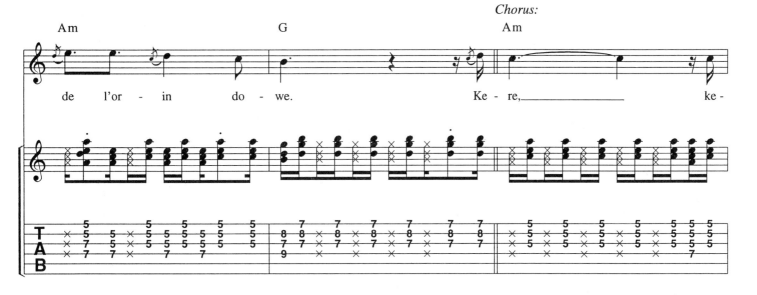

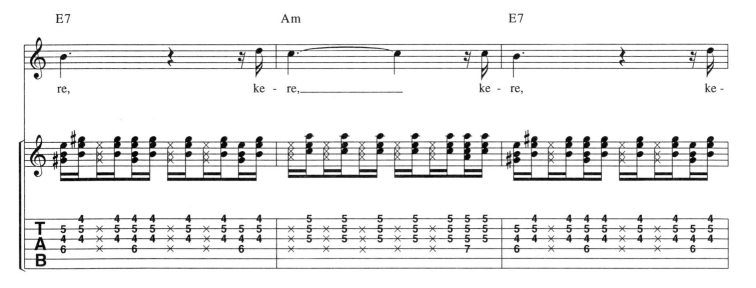

Se Eni A Fe L'Amo-Kere Kere - 16 - 4
PG9540

*Gtr. 1 plays Em.

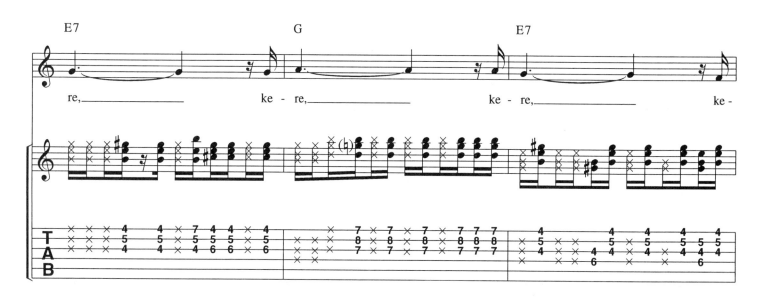

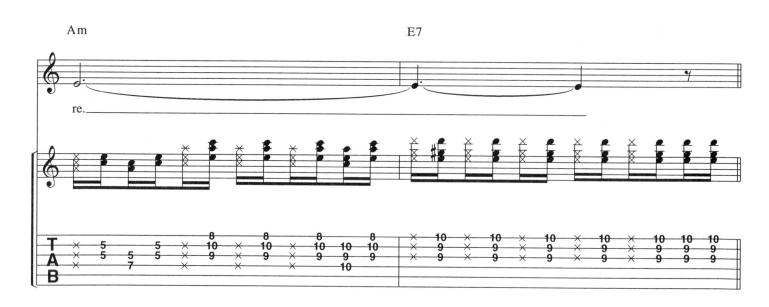

Se Eni A Fe L'Amo-Kere Kere - 16 - 5
PG9540

54

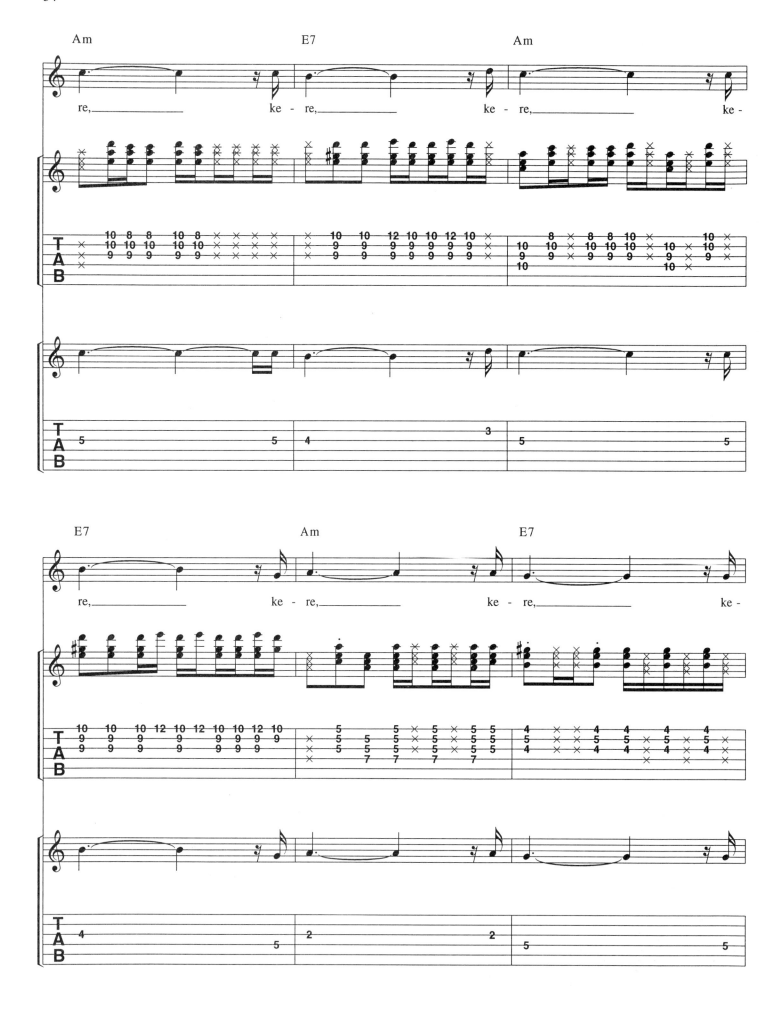

56

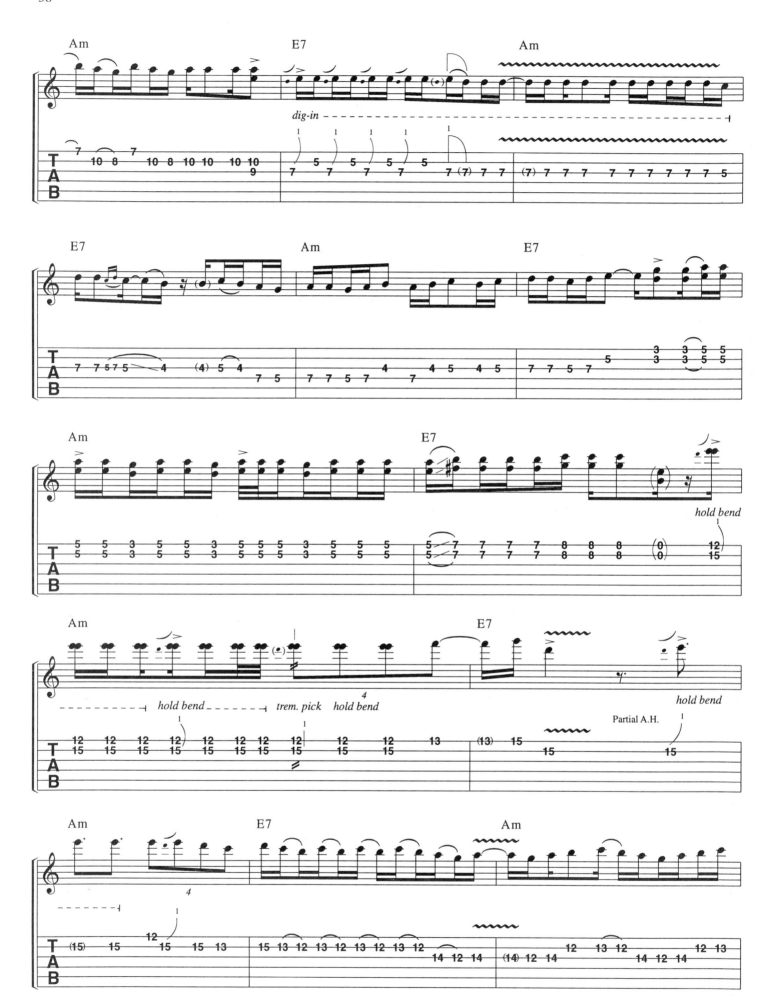

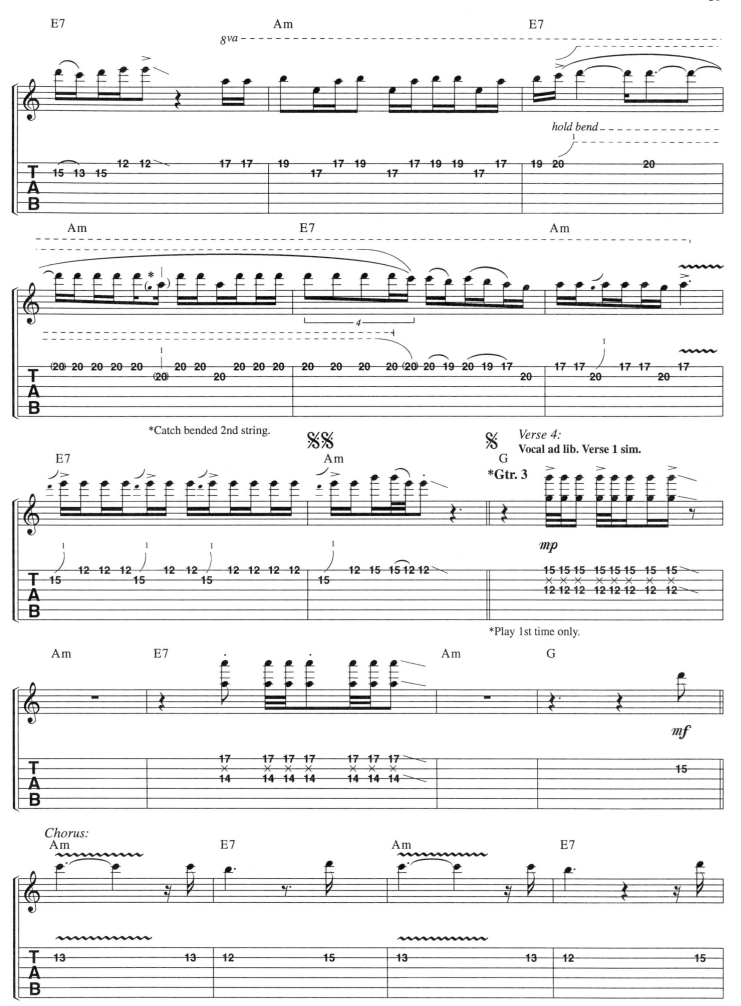

*Catch bended 2nd string.

*Play 1st time only.

Se Eni A Fe L'Amo-Kere Kere - 16 - 12
PG9540

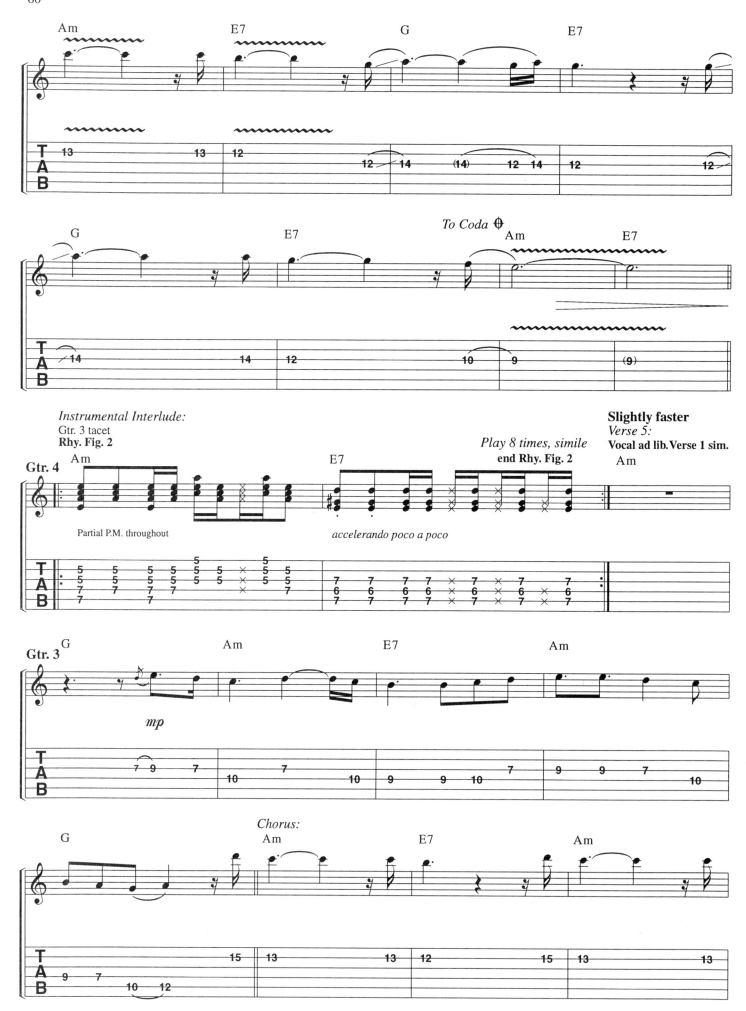

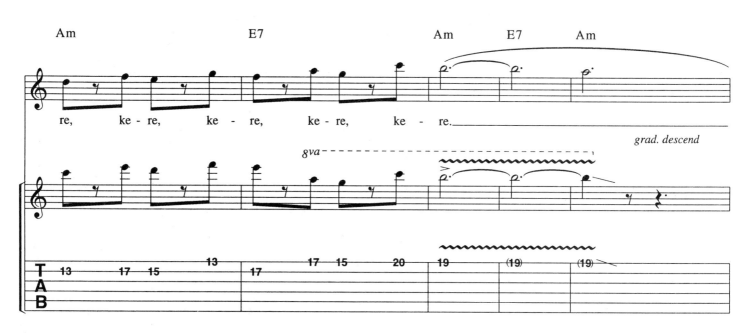

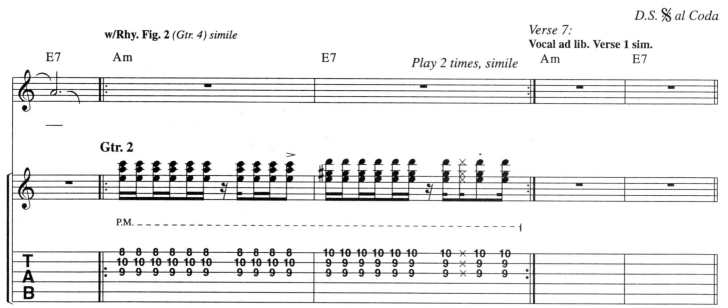

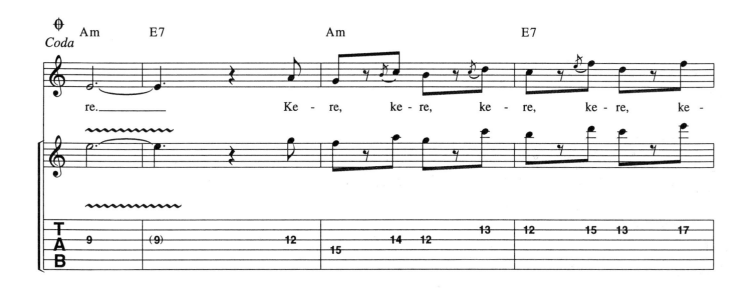

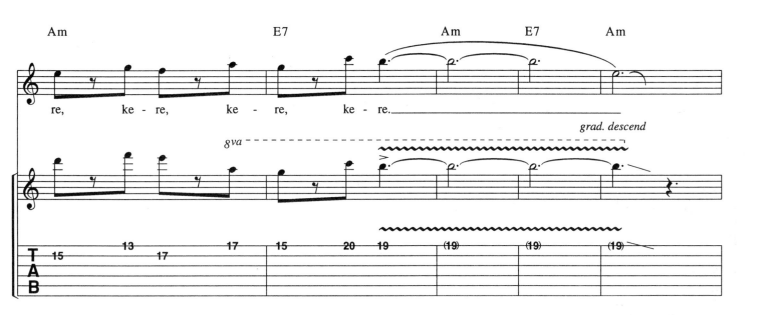

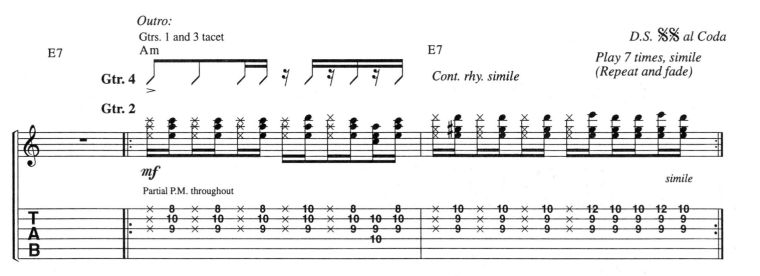

MUDBONE

Words and Music by
CARLOS SANTANA

Moderately fast ♩ = 120
Intro:
Gtr. 1 *(semi-clean, dbld. by keybd.)*

*Em

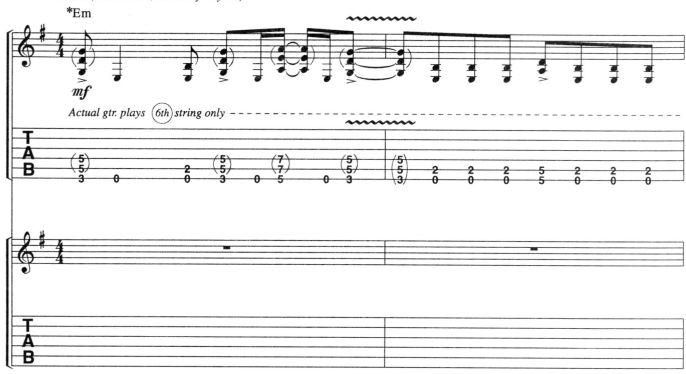

*Basic tonality of E minor.

Gtr. 2 *(w/wah effect and echo-delay throughout)*

Mudbone - 17 - 1
PG9540

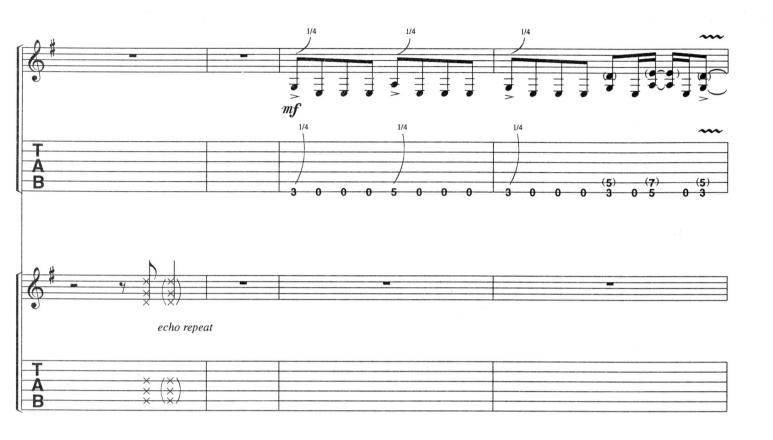

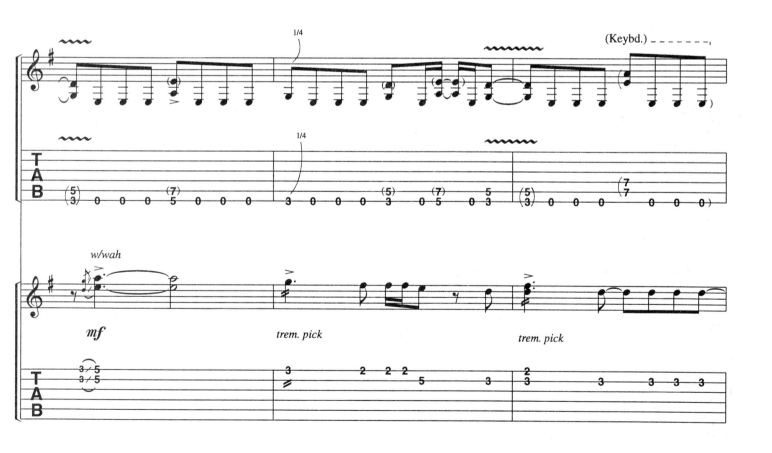

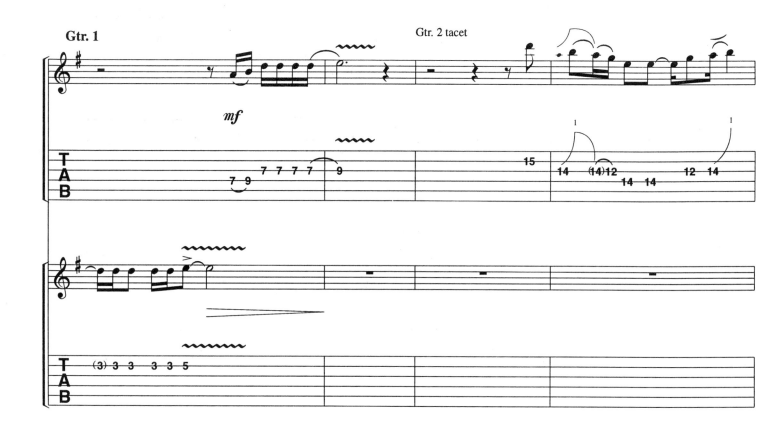

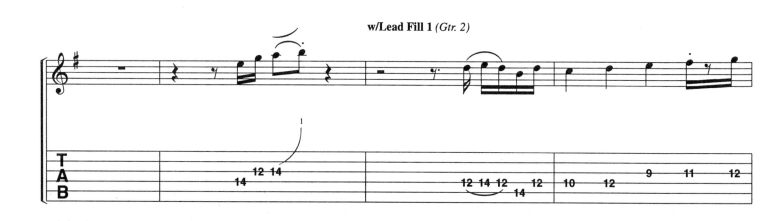

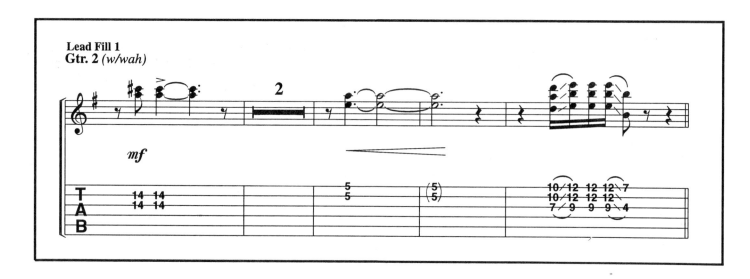

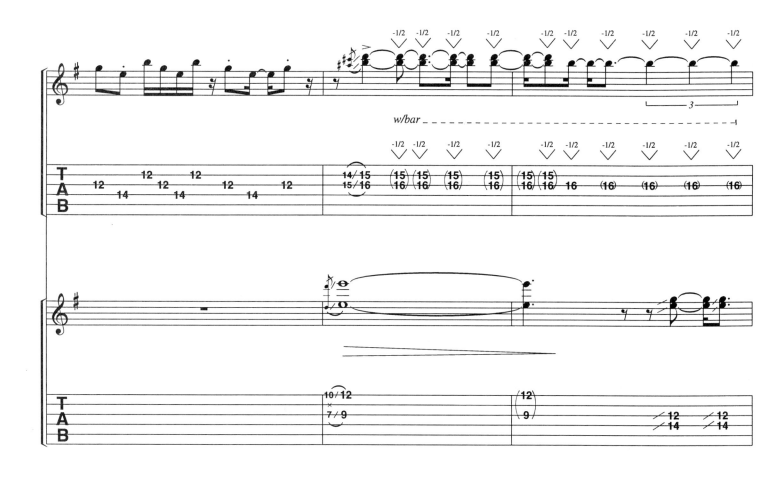

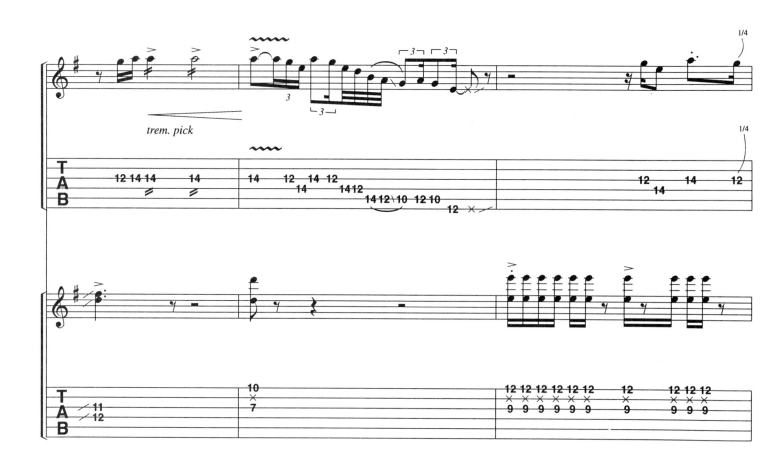

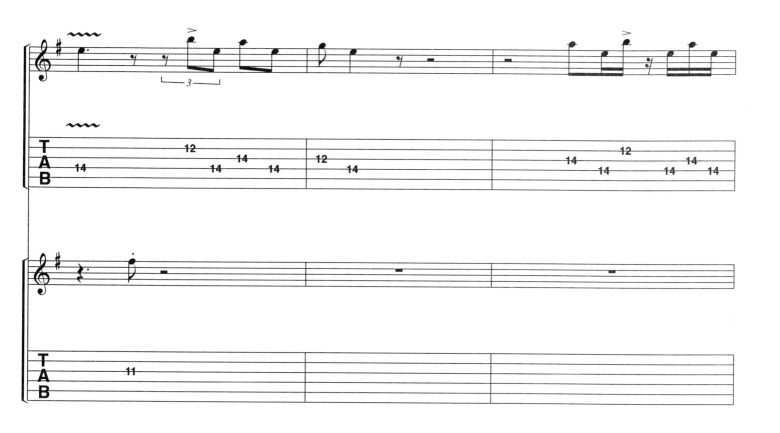

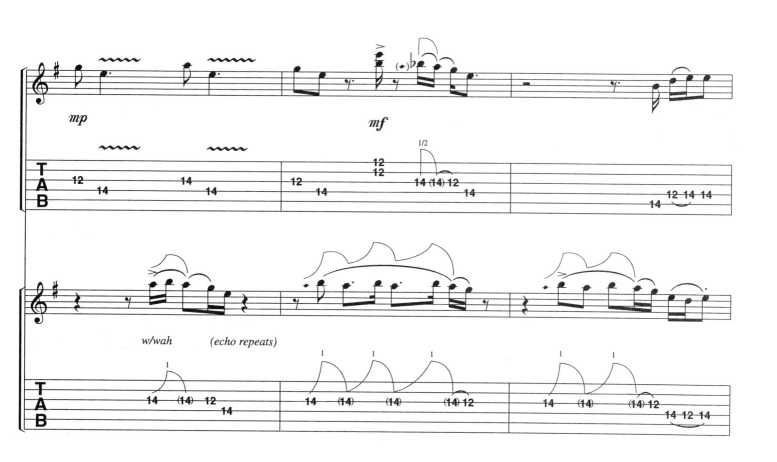

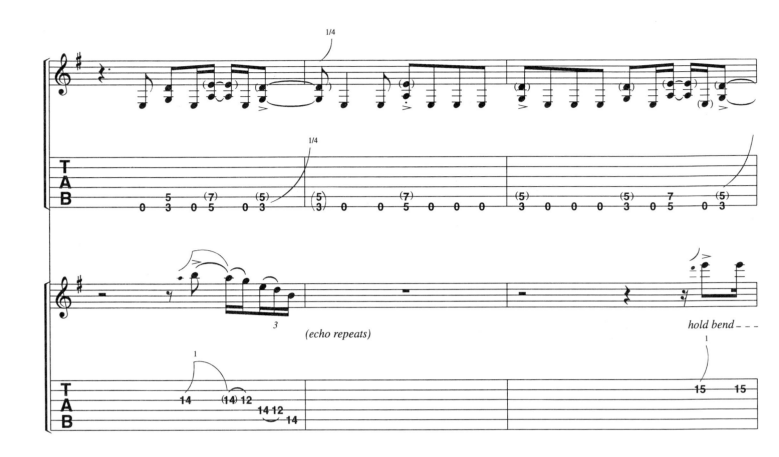

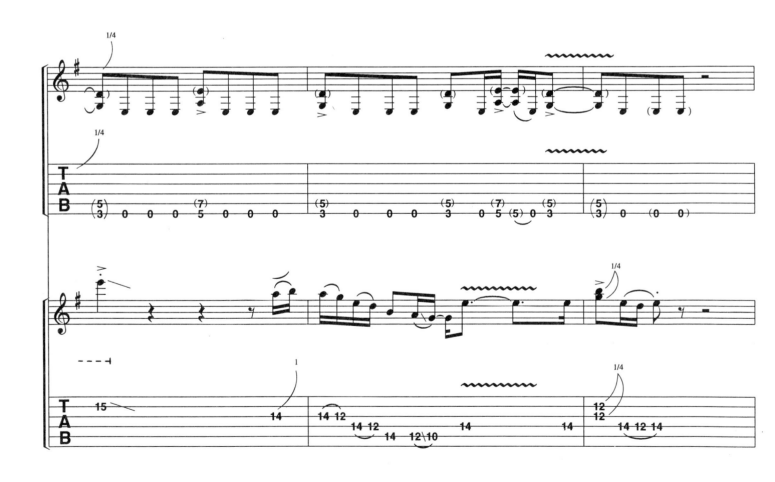

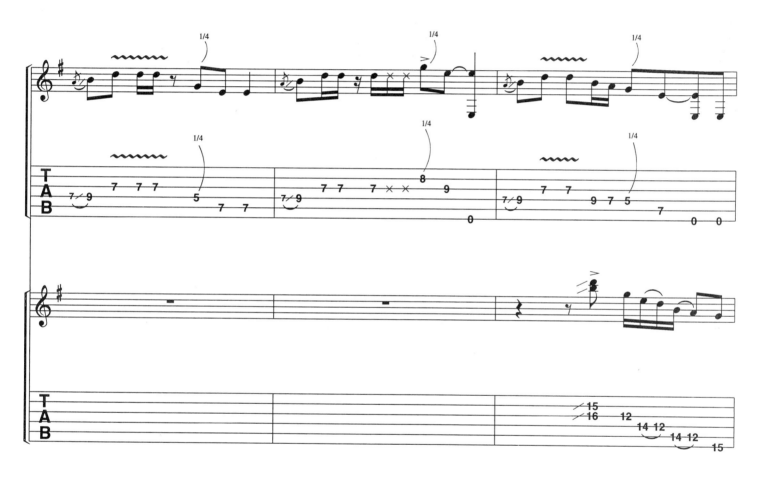

Mudbone - 17 - 8
PG9540

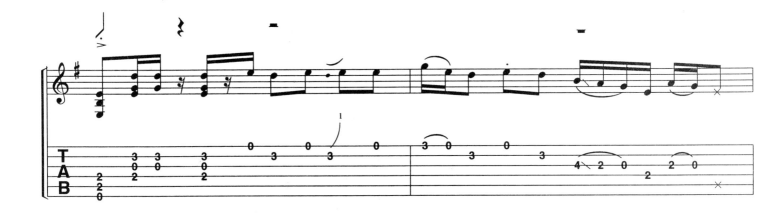

Harmonica Solo:

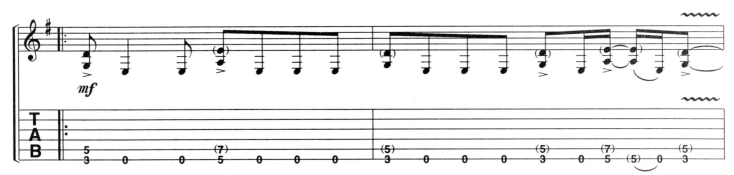

Rhy. Fig. 1   **end Rhy. Fig.1**

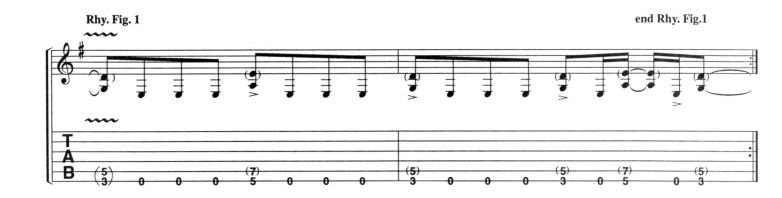

Guitar/Harmonica call/response:

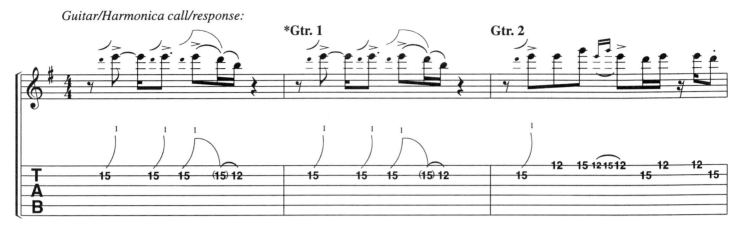

*Doubled by harmonica.

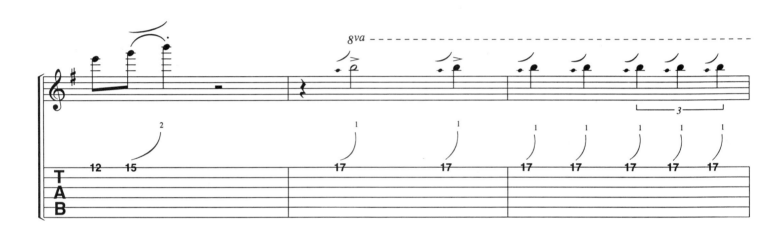

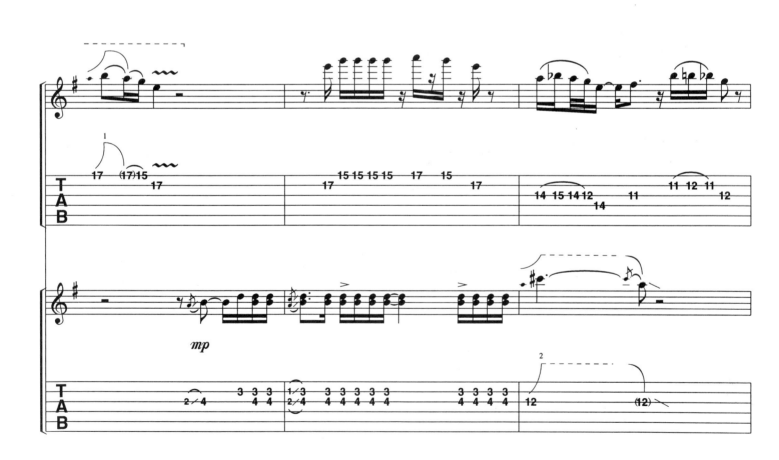

w/Rhy. **Fig. 1** *(Gtr. 3) 3 times, simile*

Gtr. 1

Guitar and Keybd. call and response:

THE HEALER

Words and Music by
CARLOS SANTANA, CHESTER THOMPSON,
ROY ROGERS and JOHN LEE HOOKER

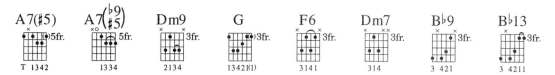

Moderately ♩ = 108
Intro:
Gtr. 1 *(Electric w/dist.)*

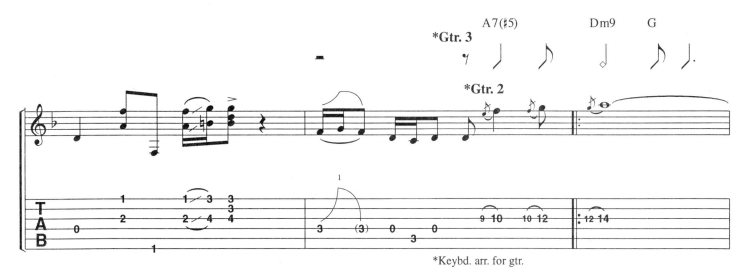

*Keybd. arr. for gtr.

The Healer - 14 - 1
PG9540

82

84

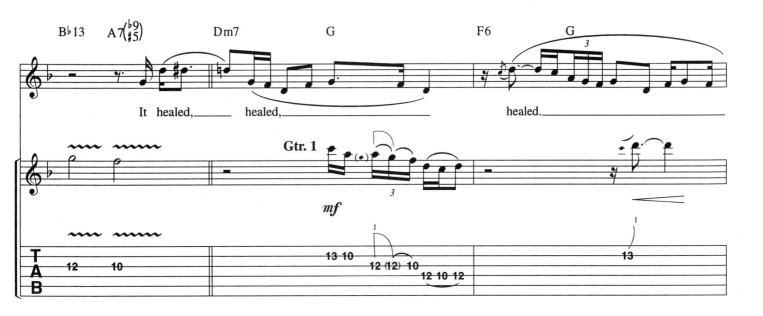

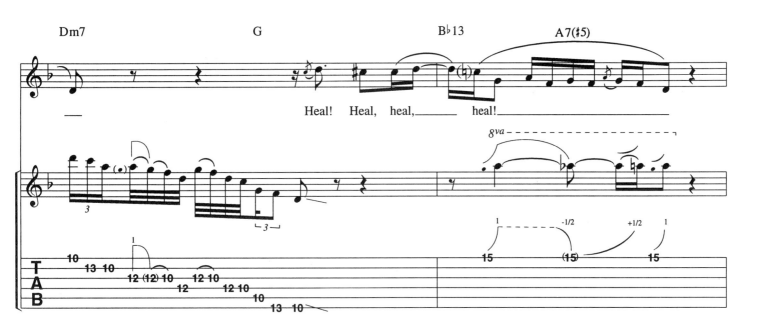

The Healer - 14 - 7
PG9540

88

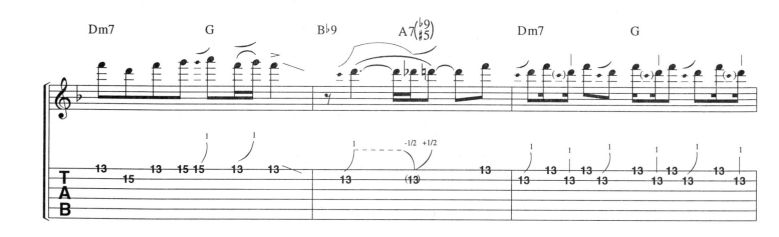

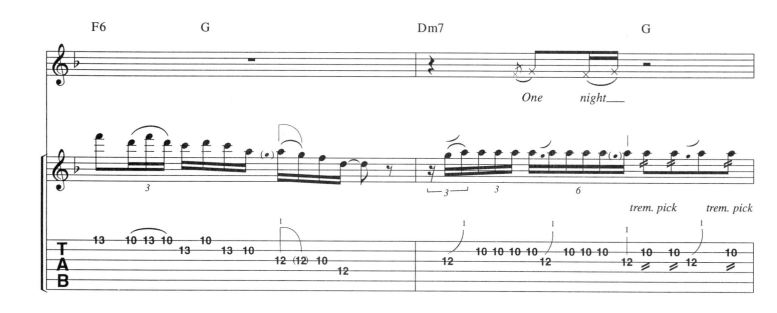

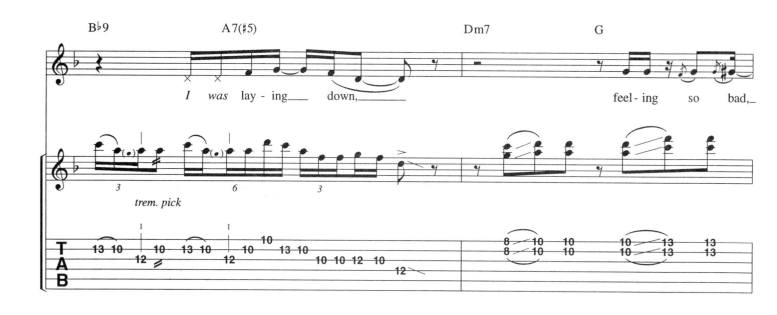

The Healer - 14 - 8
PG9540

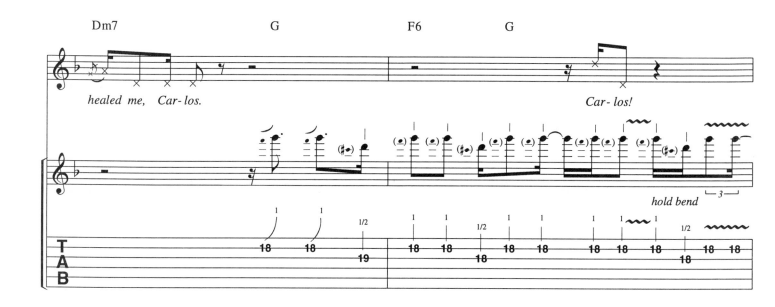

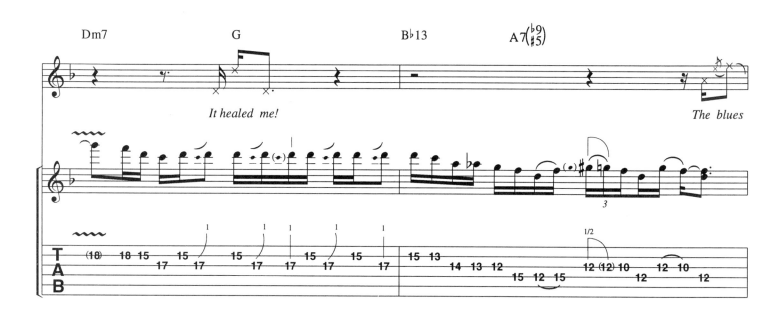

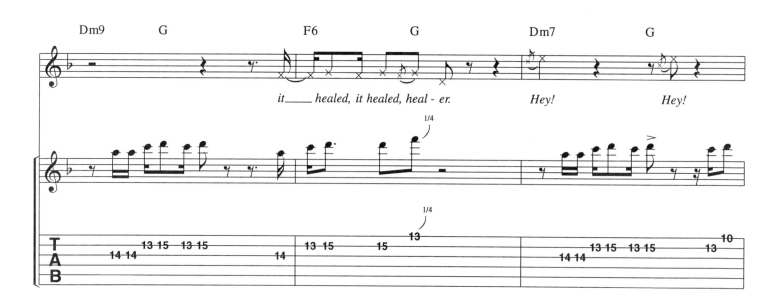

90

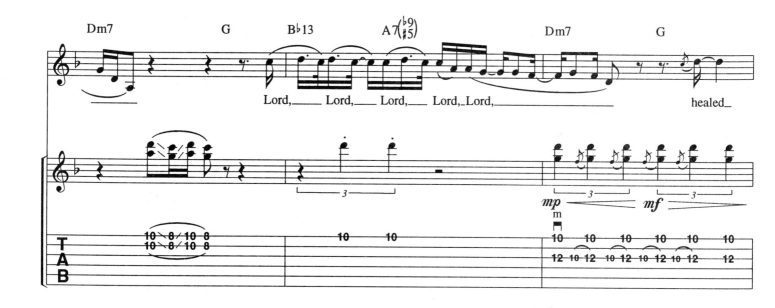

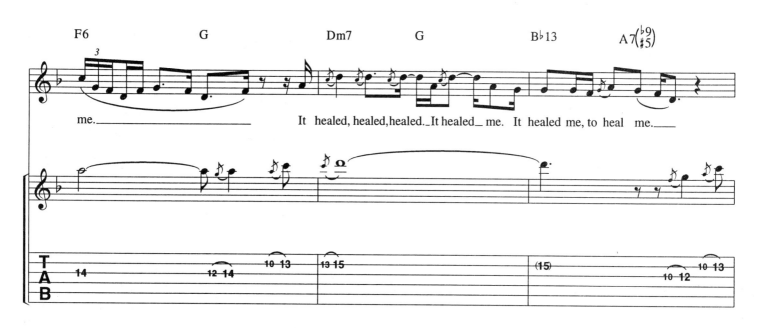

CHILL OUT (THINGS GONNA CHANGE)

Words and Music by
CARLOS SANTANA, CHESTER THOMPSON
and **JOHN LEE HOOKER**

*Keybd. arr. for fingerstyle guitar.

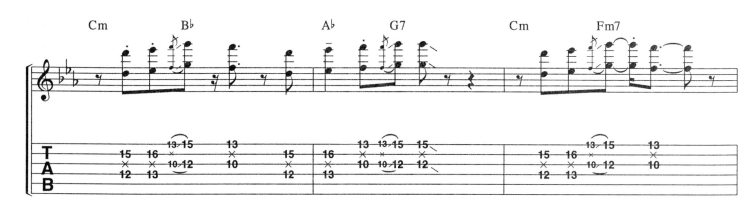

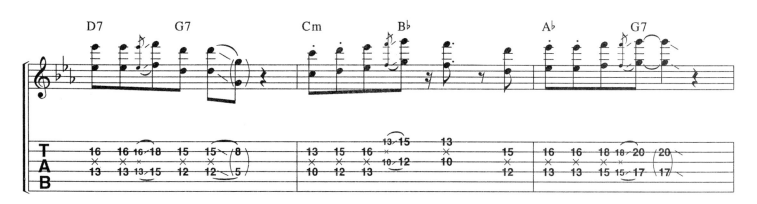

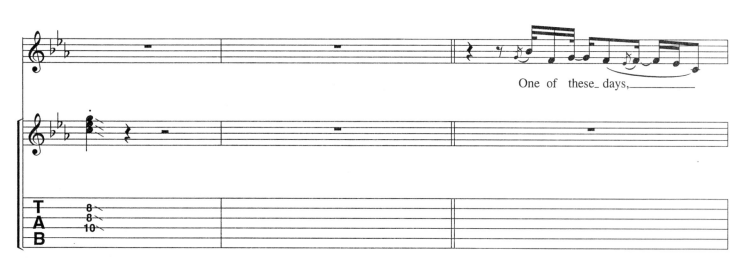

Chill Out (Things Gonna Change) - 9 - 2
PG9540

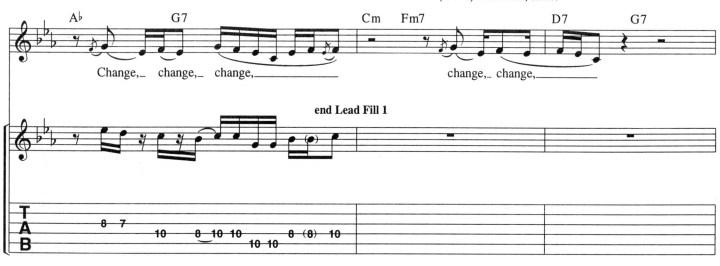

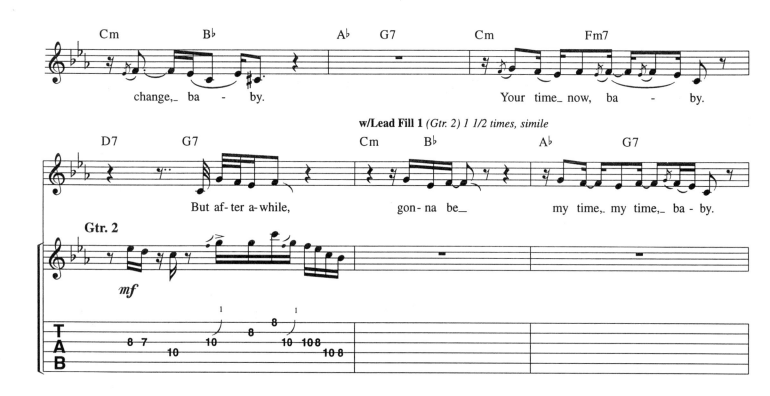

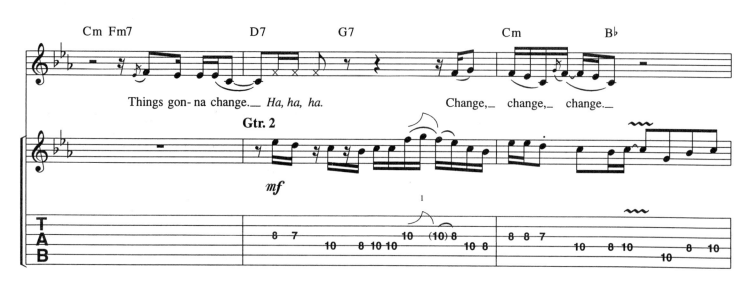

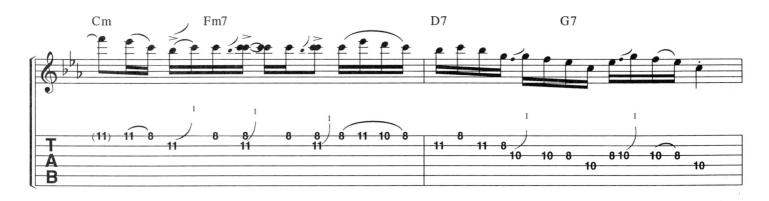

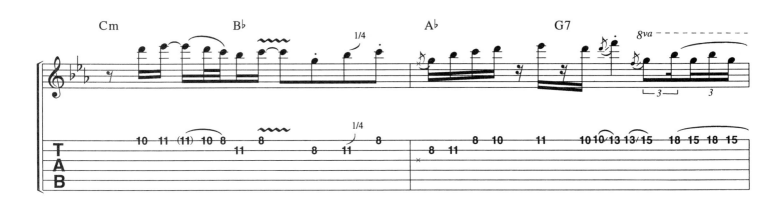

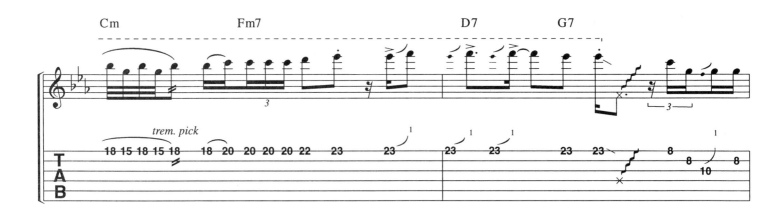

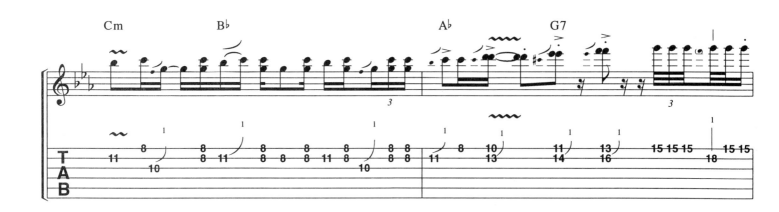

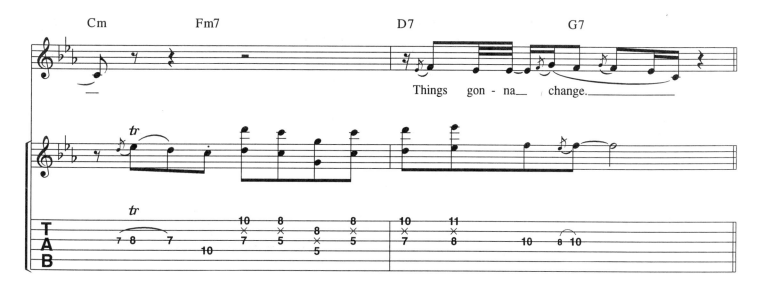

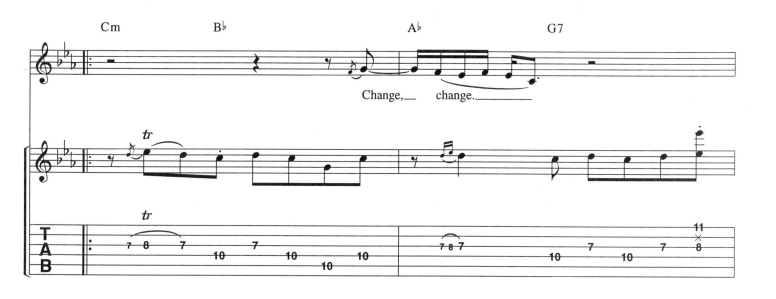

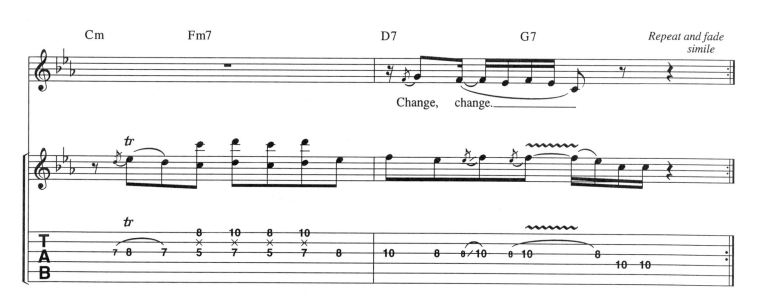

SWEET BLACK CHERRY PIE

Words and Music by
CARLOS SANTANA, CHESTER THOMPSON
and ALEX LIGERTWOOD

Sweet Black Cherry Pie - 7 - 4

PG9540

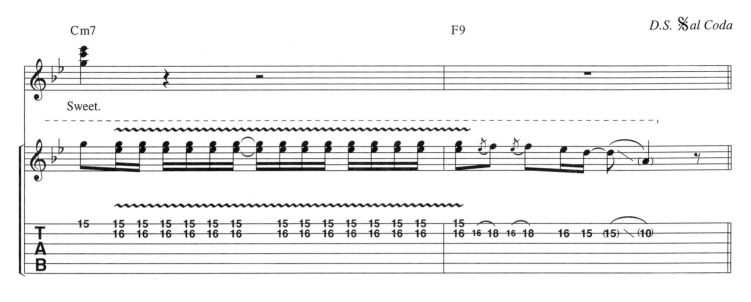

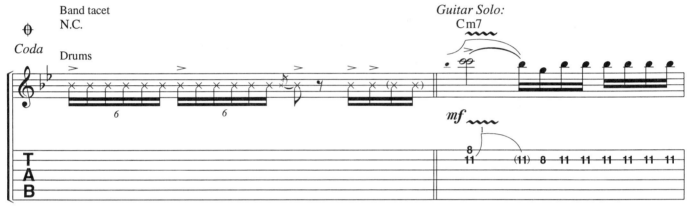

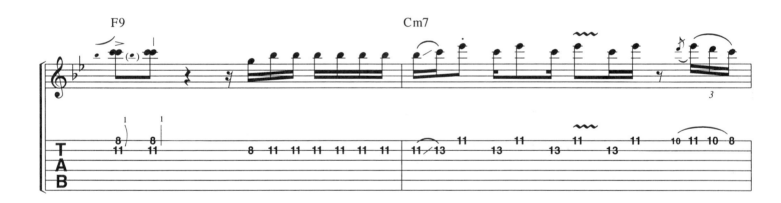

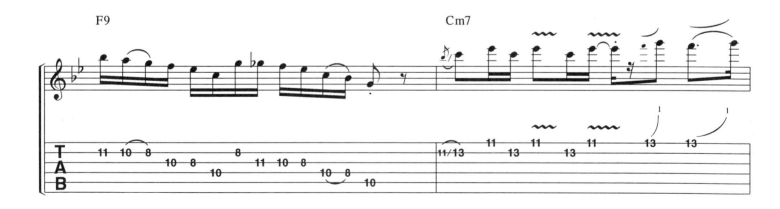

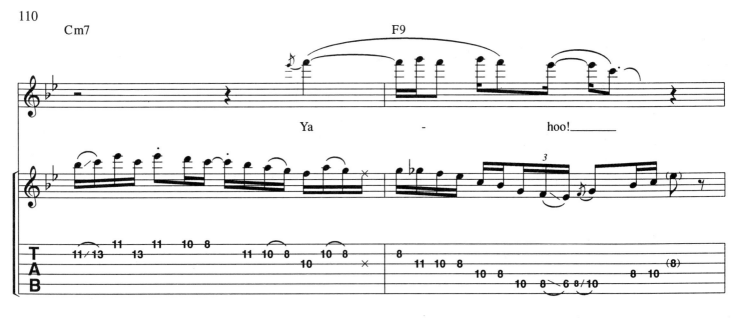

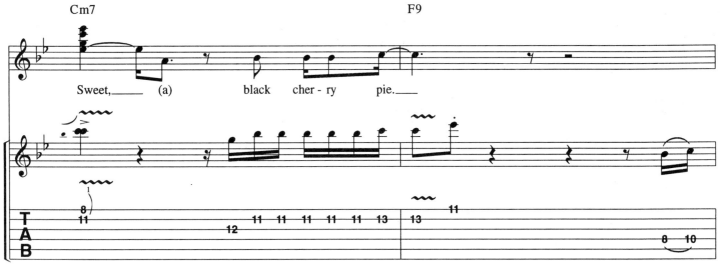

Verse 2:
My old grandma, ha, ha, she used to swing.
Making that dough and doing her thing.
She had a tree in her backyard.
When we were kids we'd fill our dogs with...
(To Chorus:)

Verse 3:
Everybody get together, let's have some fun.
Stay up all night and welcome the sun.
I've got to find my favorite treat.
No, not tomorrow, got to fill that need for...
(To Chorus:)

EVERY NOW AND THEN

By VERNON REID

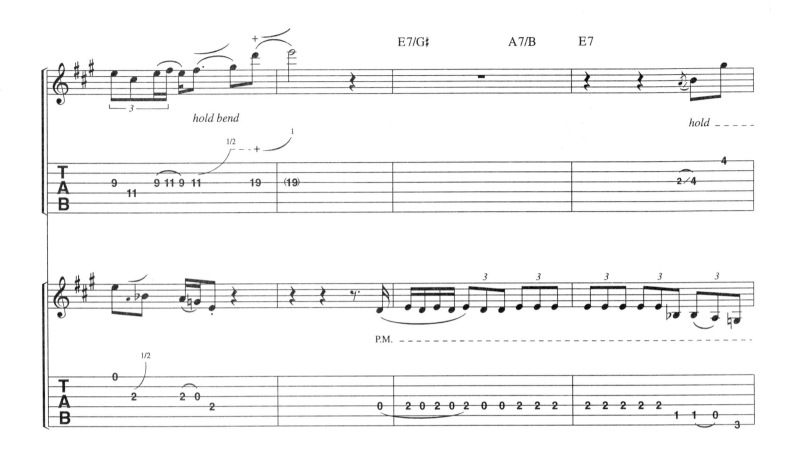

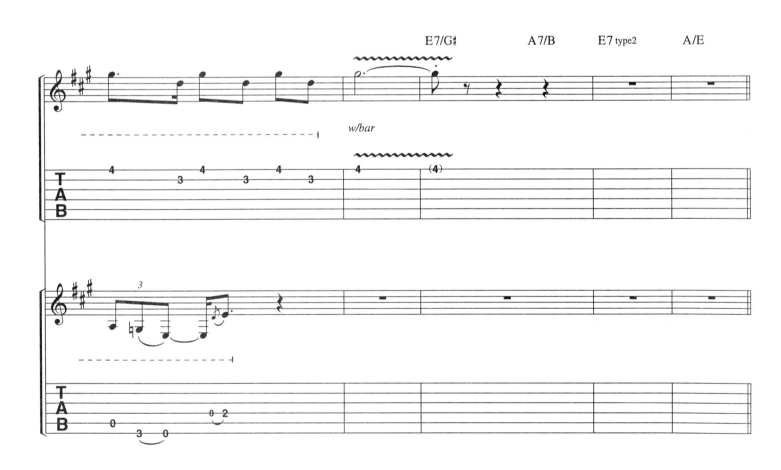

*Keyboard.

114

Every Now and Then - 19 - 4
PG9540

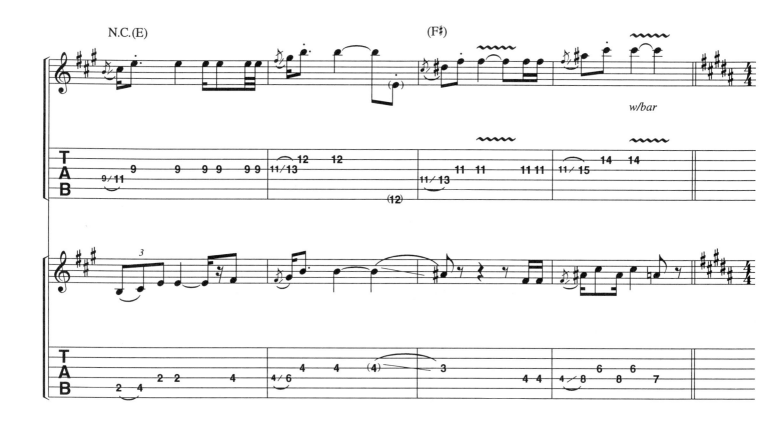

Slightly faster ♩ = 122

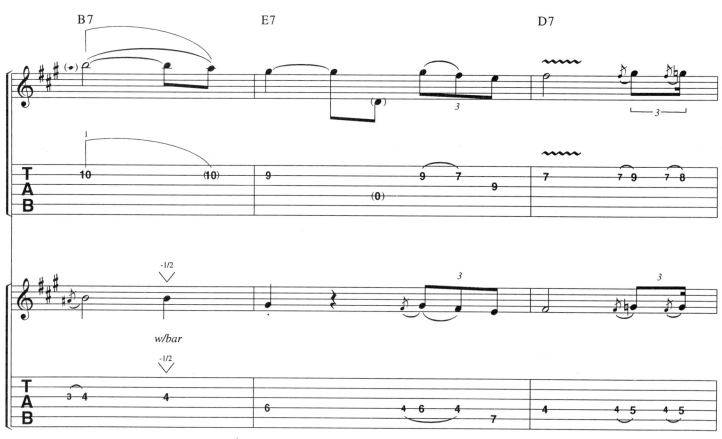

122

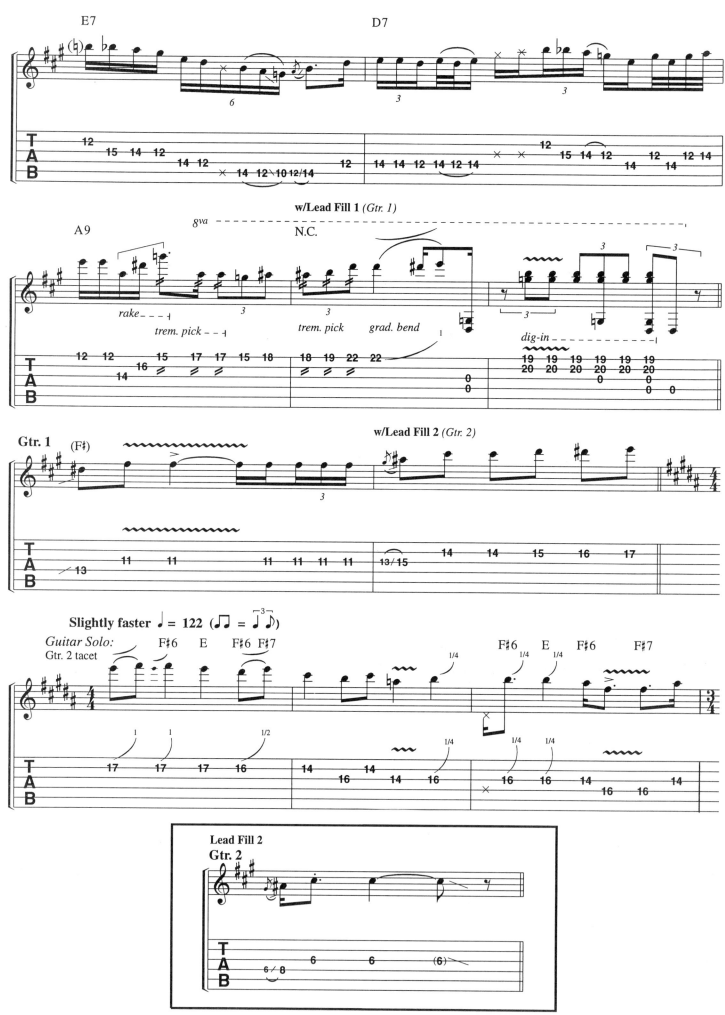

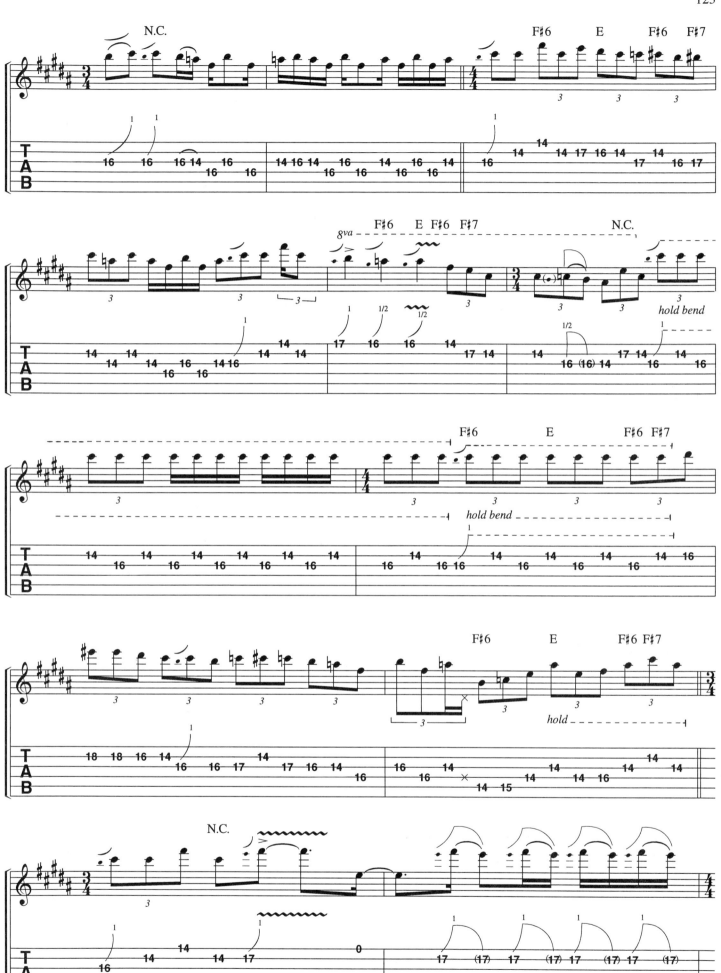

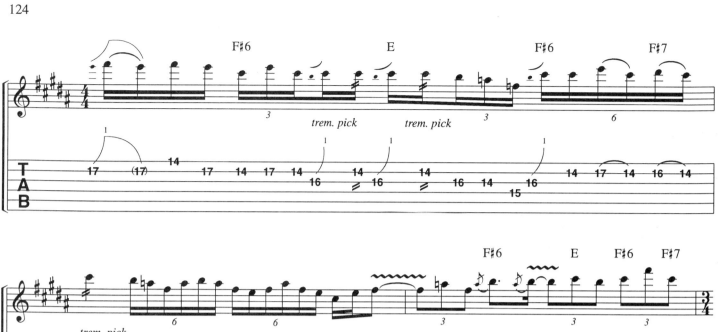

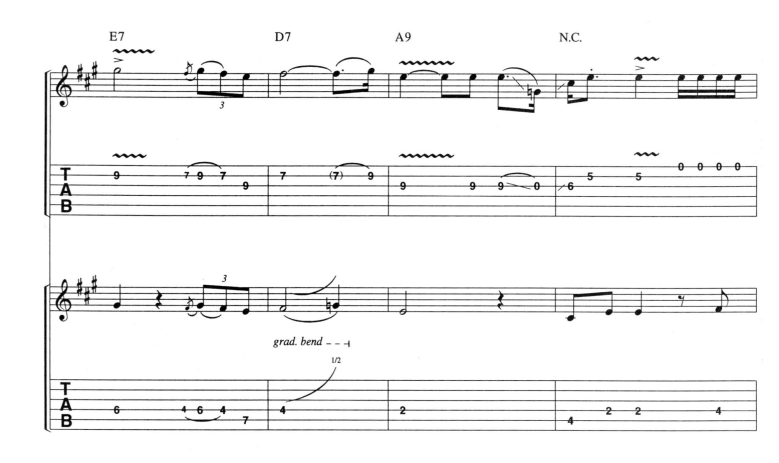

Outro:

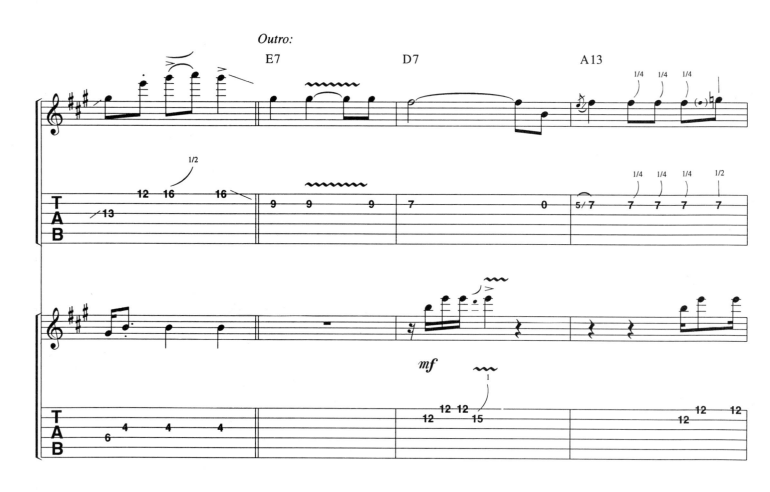

128

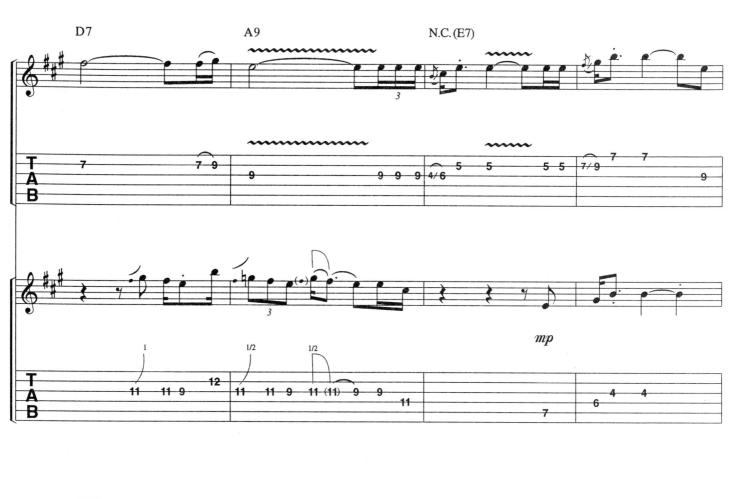

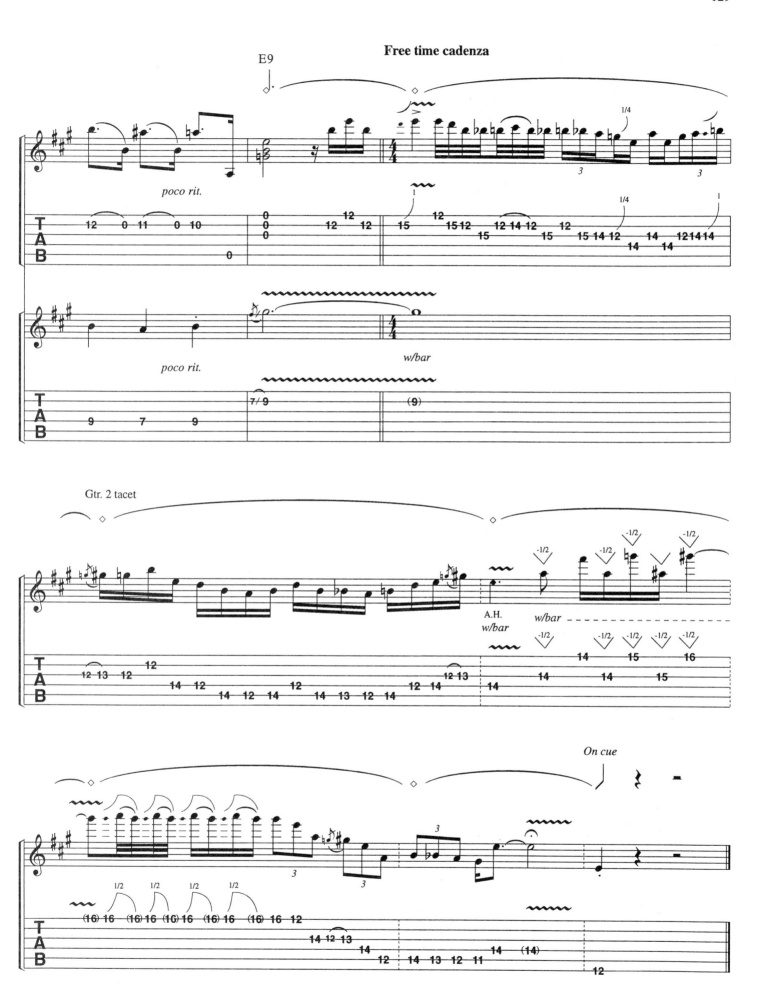

THIS IS THIS

By JOSEF ZAWINUL

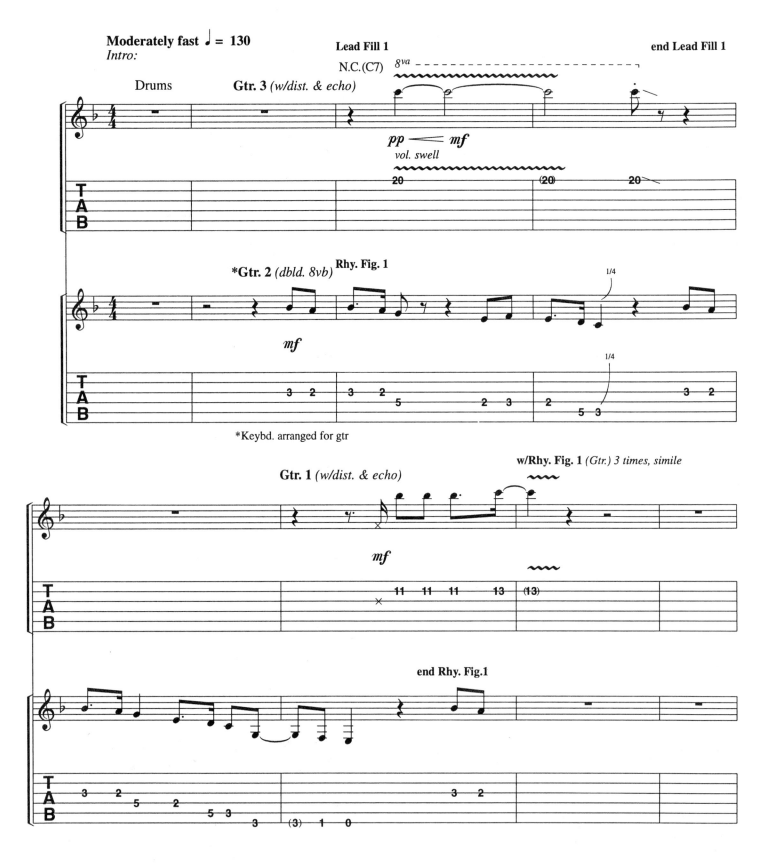

This Is This - 20 - 1
PG9540

N.C.(C7)

w/vcl. ad lib.

Gtr. 2

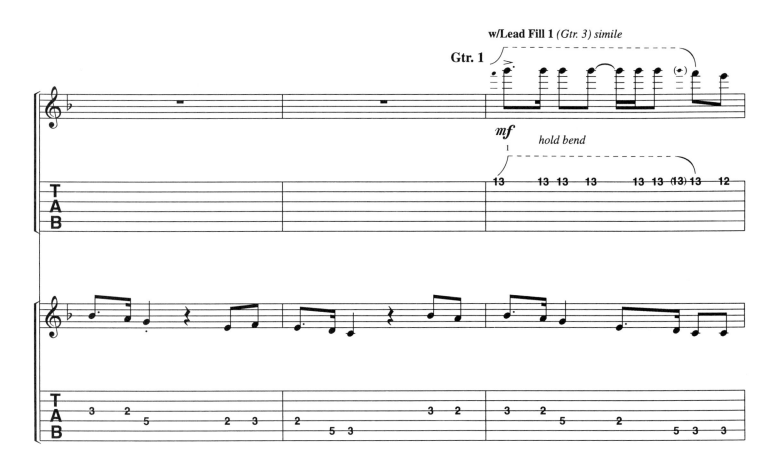

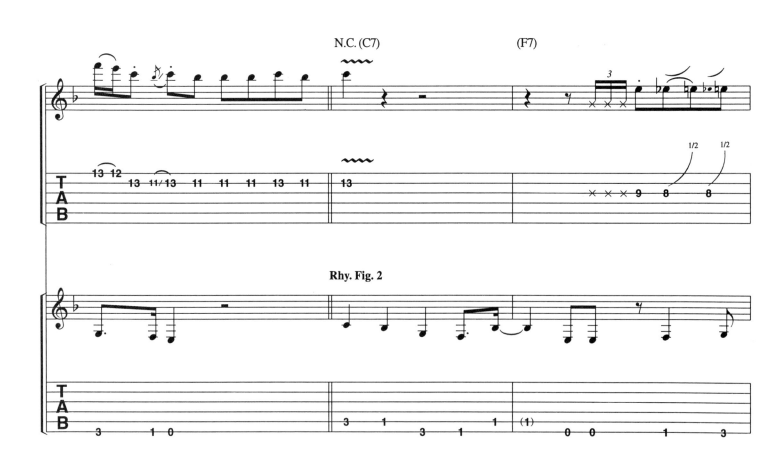

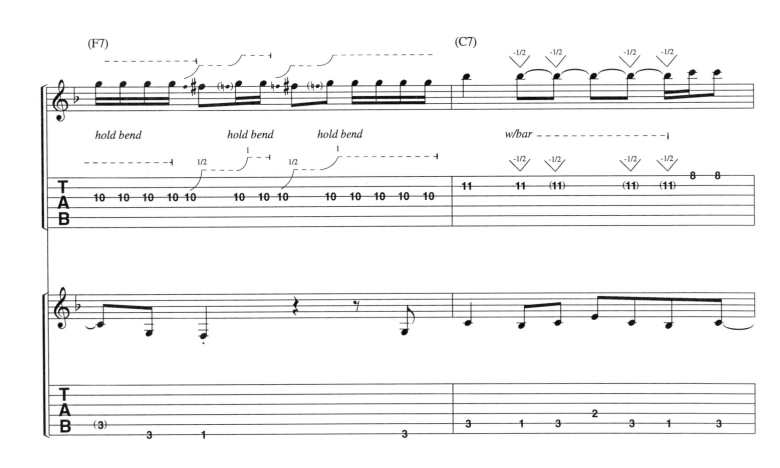

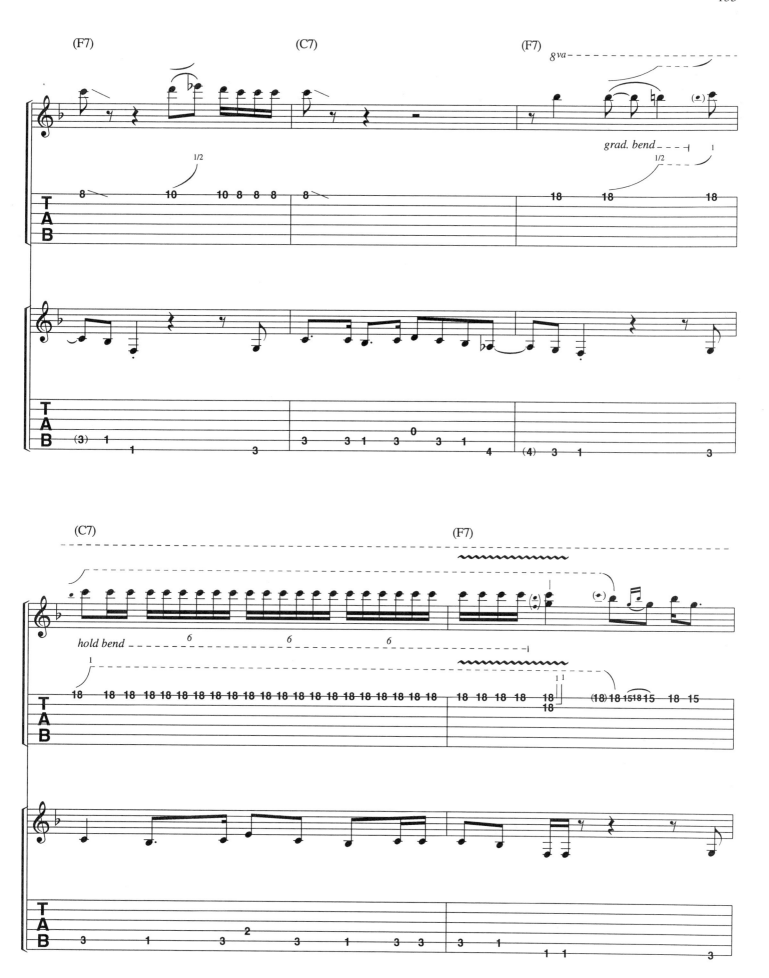

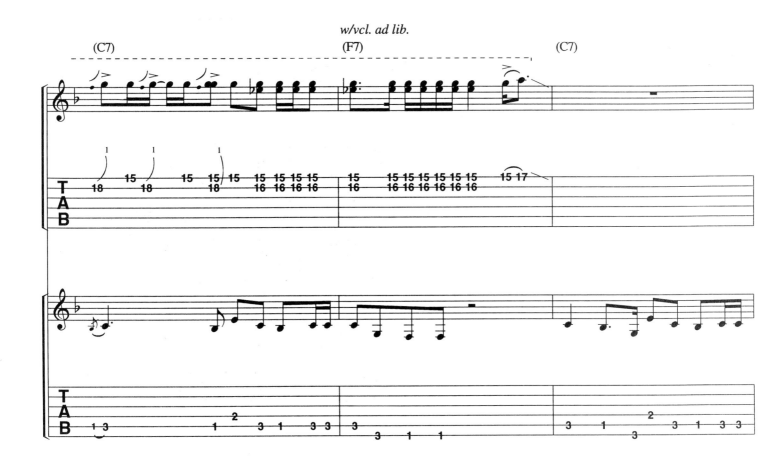

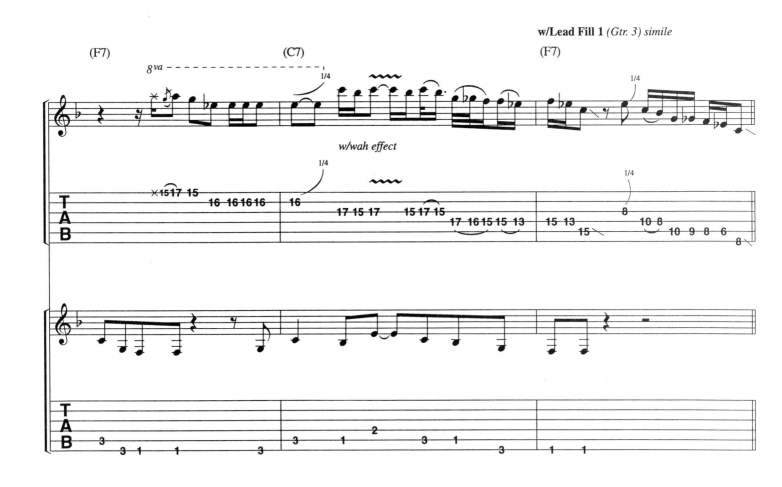

138

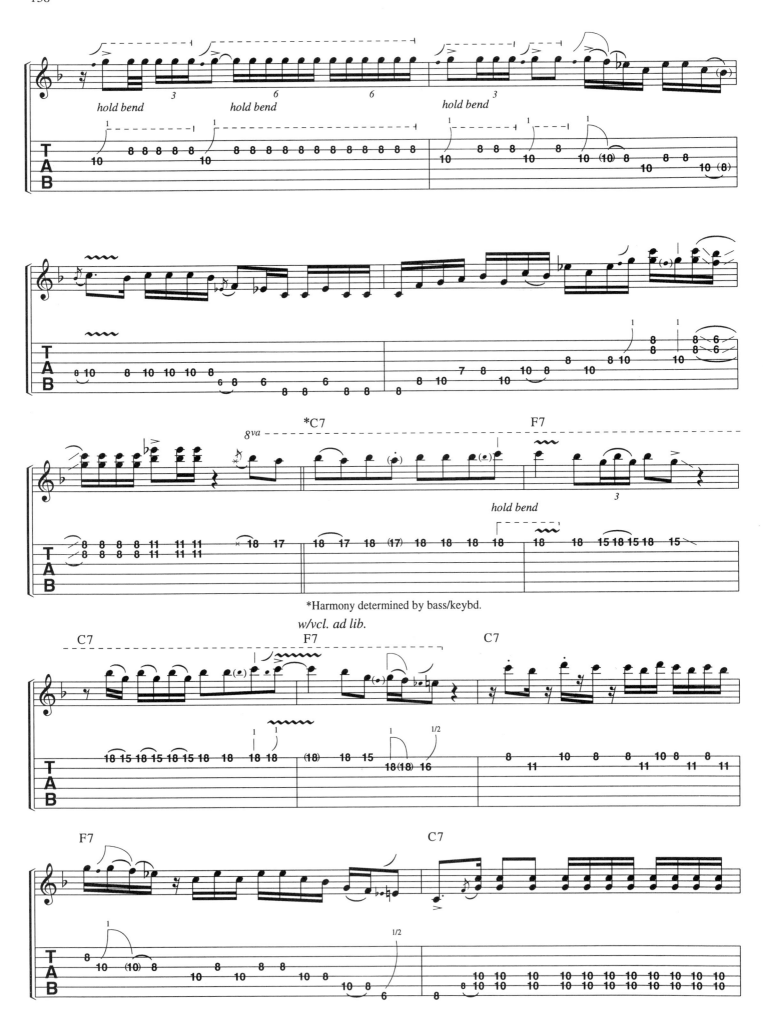

*Harmony determined by bass/keybd.

w/vcl. ad lib.

This Is This - 20 - 9
PG9540

140

This Is This - 20 - 11
PG9540

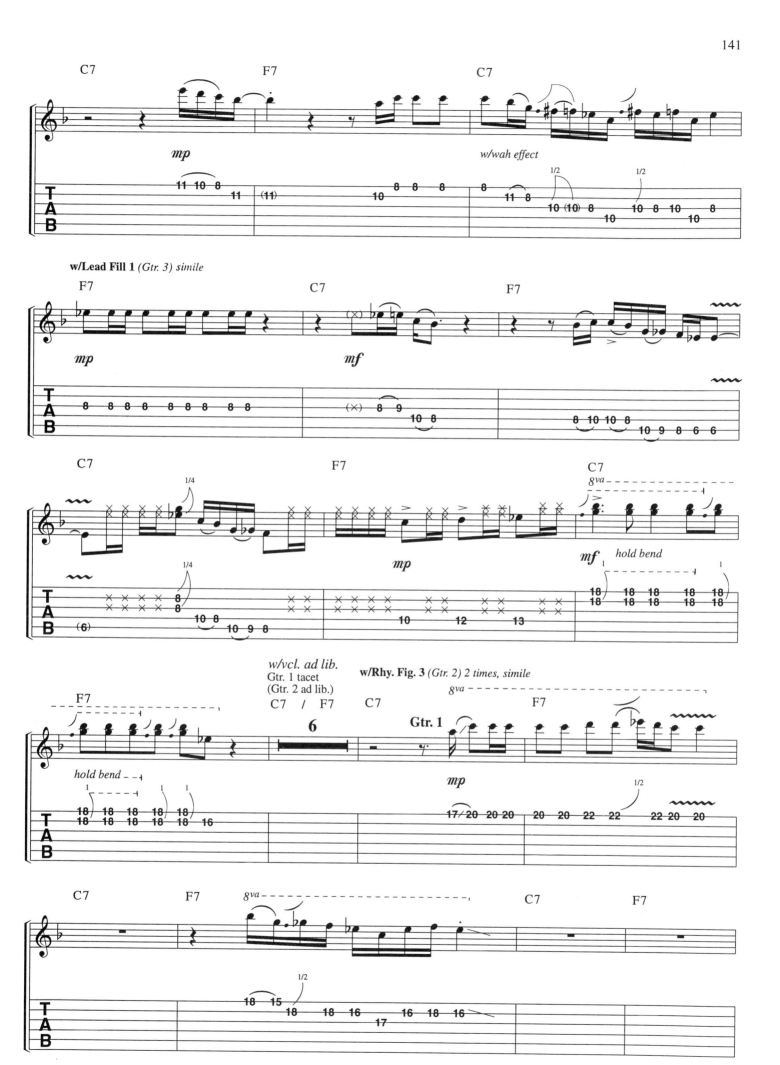

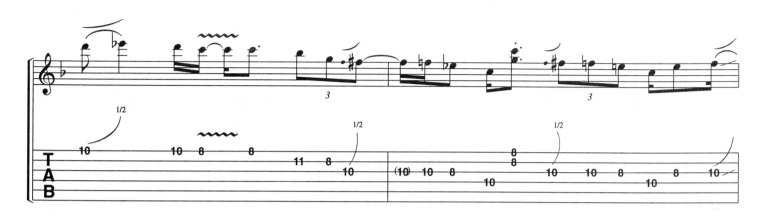

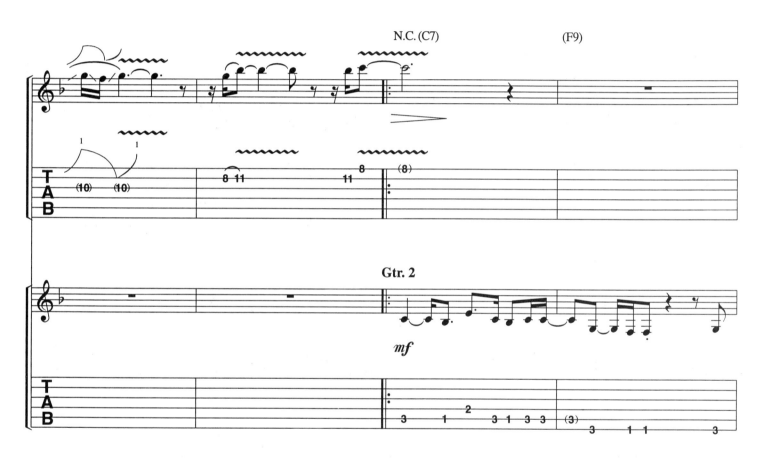

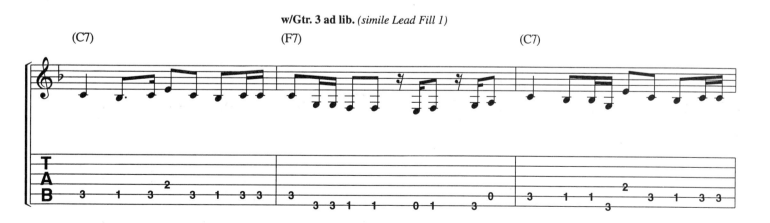

144

146

This Is This - 20 - 17
PG9540

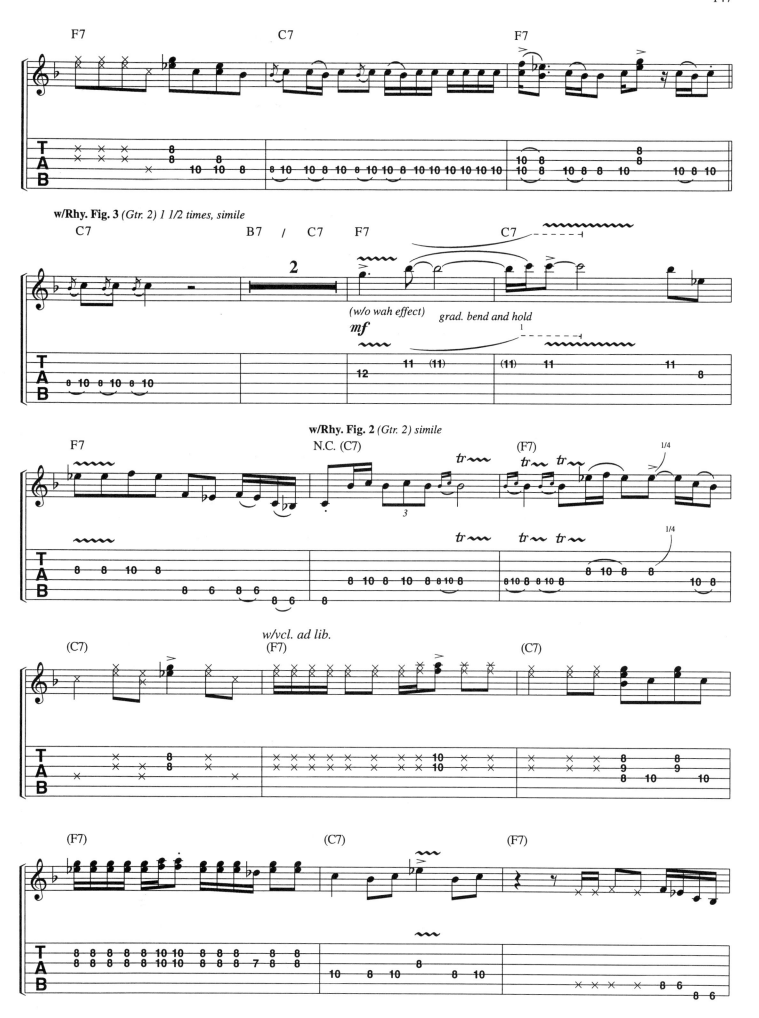

This Is This - 20 - 18
PG9540

148

This Is This - 20 - 19
PG9540

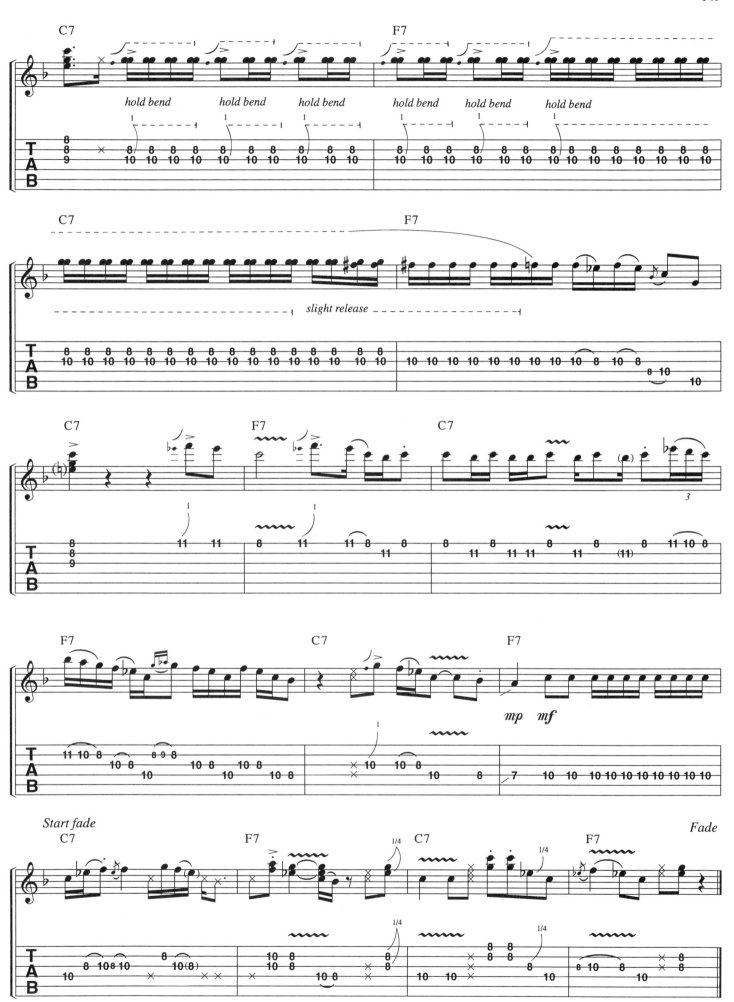

This Is This - 20 - 20
PG9540

GUITAR TAB GLOSSARY **

TABLATURE EXPLANATION

READING TABLATURE: Tablature illustrates the six strings of the guitar. Notes and chords are indicated by the placement of fret numbers on a given string(s).

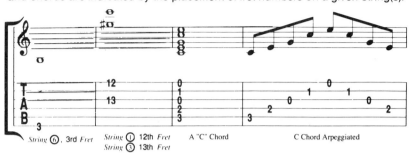

String ⑥, 3rd *Fret*   String ① 12th *Fret*   A "C" Chord   C Chord Arpeggiated
String ③ 13th *Fret*

BENDING NOTES

HALF STEP: Play the note and bend string one half step.*

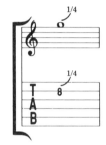

SLIGHT BEND (Microtone): Play the note and bend string slightly to the equivalent of half a fret.

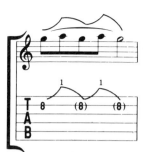

BEND AND RELEASE: Play the note and gradually bend to the next pitch, then release to the original note. Only the first note is attacked.

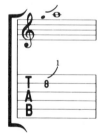

WHOLE STEP: Play the note and bend string one whole step.

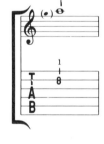

PREBEND (Ghost Bend): Bend to the specified note, before the string is picked.

BENDS INVOLVING MORE THAN ONE STRING: Play the note and bend string while playing an additional note (or notes) on another string(s). Upon release, relieve pressure from additional note(s), causing original note to sound alone.

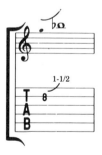

WHOLE STEP AND A HALF: Play the note and bend string a whole step and a half.

PREBEND AND RELEASE: Bend the string, play it, then release to the original note.

BENDS INVOLVING STATIONARY NOTES: Play notes and bend lower pitch, then hold until release begins (indicated at the point where line becomes solid).

UNISON BEND: Play both notes and immediately bend the lower note to the same pitch as the higher note.

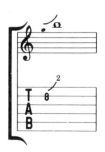

TWO STEPS: Play the note and bend string two whole steps.

REVERSE BEND: Play the already-bent string, then immediately drop it down to the fretted note.

DOUBLE NOTE BEND: Play both notes and immediately bend both strings simultaneously.

*A half step is the smallest interval in Western music; it is equal to one fret. A whole step equals two frets.

© 1990 Beam Me Up Music
c/o CPP/Belwin, Inc. Miami, Florida 33014
International Copyright Secured   Made in U.S.A.   All Rights Reserved   **By Kenn Chipkin and Aaron Stang

RHYTHM SLASHES

STRUM INDICA-TIONS: Strum with indicated rhythm.

The chord voicings are found on the first page of the transcription underneath the song title.

INDICATING SINGLE NOTES USING RHYTHM SLASHES: Very often single notes are incorporated into a rhythm part. The note name is indicated above the rhythm slash with a fret number and a string indication.

ARTICULATIONS

HAMMER ON: Play lower note, then "hammer on" to higher note with another finger. Only the first note is attacked.

LEFT HAND HAMMER: Hammer on the first note played on each string with the left hand.

PULL OFF: Play higher note, then "pull off" to lower note with another finger. Only the first note is attacked.

FRET-BOARD TAPPING: "Tap" onto the note indicated by + with a finger of the pick hand, then pull off to the following note held by the fret hand.

TAP SLIDE: Same as fretboard tapping, but the tapped note is slid randomly up the fretboard, then pulled off to the following note.

BEND AND TAP TECHNIQUE: Play note and bend to specified interval. While holding bend, tap onto note indicated.

LEGATO SLIDE: Play note and slide to the following note. (Only first note is attacked).

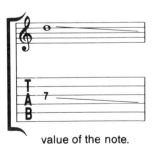

LONG GLISSAN-DO: Play note and slide in specified direction for the full value of the note.

SHORT GLISSAN-DO: Play note for its full value and slide in specified direction at the last possible moment.

PICK SLIDE: Slide the edge of the pick in specified direction across the length of the string(s).

MUTED STRINGS: A percussive sound is made by laying the fret hand across all six strings while pick hand strikes specified area (low, mid, high strings).

PALM MUTE: The note or notes are muted by the palm of the pick hand by lightly touching the string(s) near the bridge.

TREMOLO PICKING: The note or notes are picked as fast as possible.

TRILL: Hammer on and pull off consecutively and as fast as possible between the original note and the grace note.

ACCENT: Notes or chords are to be played with added emphasis.

STACCATO (Detached Notes): Notes or chords are to be played roughly half their actual value and with separation.

DOWN STROKES AND UPSTROKES: Notes or chords are to be played with either a downstroke (⊓) or upstroke (∨) of the pick.

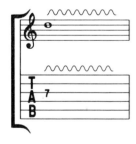

VIBRATO: The pitch of a note is varied by a rapid shaking of the fret hand finger, wrist, and forearm.

HARMONICS

NATURAL HARMONIC: A finger of the fret hand lightly touches the note or notes indicated in the tab and is played by the pick hand.

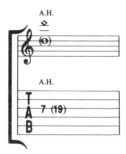

ARTIFICIAL HARMONIC: The first tab number is fretted, then the pick hand produces the harmonic by using a finger to lightly touch the same string at the second tab number (in parenthesis) and is then picked by another finger.

ARTIFICIAL "PINCH" HARMONIC: A note is fretted as indicated by the tab, then the pick hand produces the harmonic by squeezing the pick firmly while using the tip of the index finger in the pick attack. If parenthesis are found around the fretted note, it does not sound. No parenthesis means both the fretted note and A.H. are heard simultaneously.

TREMOLO BAR

SPECIFIED INTERVAL: The pitch of a note or chord is lowered to a specified interval and then may or may not return to the original pitch. The activity of the tremolo bar is graphically represented by peaks and valleys.

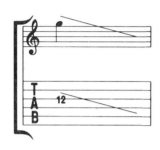

UN-SPECIFIED INTERVAL: The pitch of a note or a chord is lowered to an unspecified interval.